Creative Ideas for Pastoral Liturgy

FUNERAL, MEMORIAL and THANKSGIVING SERVICES

Creative Ideas for Pastoral Liturgy

Funeral, Memorial and Thanksgiving Services

Jan Brind and Tessa Wilkinson

CANTERBURY
PRESS
Norwich

© Jan Brind and Tessa Wilkinson 2008

First published in 2008 by the Canterbury Press Norwich
(a publishing imprint of Hymns Ancient & Modern Limited,
a registered charity)
13–17 Long Lane, London EC1A 9PN

www.scm-canterburypress.co.uk

Second impression

The Authors have asserted their rights under the Copyright, Designs
and Patents Act, 1988, to be identified as the Authors of this Work

British Library Cataloguing in Publication data

A catalogue record for this book is available
from the British Library

ISBN 978-1-85311-855-5

Typeset by Regent Typesetting, London
Printed and bound by
Biddles Ltd, King's Lynn, Norfolk

This book is dedicated to those we have loved
and who died tragically and left us too soon

Rob, Jo and Jamie

CONTENTS

INTRODUCTION

When someone dies, usually only a few people are present – the person's nearest relatives and maybe certain significant people in that person's life. It is at a funeral, memorial or thanksgiving service that the wider circle of the person's family and friends gather together. At a funeral we say goodbye, celebrate the person's life and commend her or him to the love and care of God. At a memorial or thanksgiving service we remember and celebrate the person's life.

We have most probably all attended many funerals and memorial or thanksgiving services. Some may have been beautifully crafted, presented and planned to reflect what was happening and celebrate the person's life or express sadness for a life cut short, while others may have been quite the reverse, with apparently no planning or carefully considered thought. For example, consider the burial of a child when the priest arrived late. The family in this instance had to stand around in the rain, and when the priest did eventually show up he didn't even know the name of the child who had died. This is inexcusable. When a family is grieving it is hard enough without having to add an additional layer of anger and pain caused by the way the burial was conducted. This is an extreme example – and hopefully rare.

'Saying goodbye well' is what we hope this book will help people to do. A funeral or memorial service gives a real opportunity for the Church to reach out and help people in their time of need. The supplementary prayers, readings, hymns, songs and music that we suggest may help families plan a service that meets their specific needs and says what they really want to say. The service outlines cover a variety of pastoral situations.

Each funeral or act of rememberance is unique to the person who has died and the family who mourn their loss. While one service may feel like a real celebration, full of praise and thanksgiving for a long life well lived, another can be quiet and reflective and full of sadness. Because people die in many different ways, the circumstances of death can make a distinct mark on the shape and feel of a service. And because the body has to be disposed of quite quickly, for some people the idea of having a funeral for just family and close friends and then, later on, a service of remembrance, works well. Others decide just to have the funeral and no other service, so it is important to spend time getting it right.

Usually the family will be coming to terms with the death, and at the same time having to decide what they want to happen at the funeral. Someone once said that planning a funeral is almost like planning a wedding, except you only have a few days in which to do it, whereas with a wedding you often have months or even years.

Many people feel that funerals have to be sombre, dark affairs, where people are dressed in black, and, instead of flowers, friends are asked to contribute money to a charity. If a funeral is the result of a tragic death it may feel more appropriate to have a sombre funeral followed later by a celebration of that person's life during a service of thanksgiving. But funerals do not *have* to be sombre. Giving to a charity is, of course, very worthwhile, particularly if the charity is connected to the person who has died. But we *can* wear bright colours, and we *can* fill the church with flowers, and we *can* sing uplifting and joyful hymns and songs interspersed with more gentle ones. *(Lord, the light of your love (Shine, Jesus, shine)* by Graham Kendrick works very well at a funeral.) We can make funerals joyful and memorable occasions when the person who has died is remembered with love and thanksgiving.

We hope that the ideas suggested in this book will be an extra resource for those who help in planning a funeral, memorial or thanksgiving service. We hope it will enable those who plan services to think beyond the given, and to be creative and imaginative, so that those who need to say 'Goodbye' can do so in ways that are appropriate and memorable. Please use the resources given in any way you like – even as a pick and mix, lifting ideas from several services to put together a service which feels appropriate to your need. Please remember to credit the authors when you reproduce material in a service sheet.

The text for many of the 'Other Readings' we have chosen can be viewed on the internet, using a search engine such as Google. Searching by title, or even a single sentence, along with the writer's name, will result in a number of websites that contain the text. If you wish to reproduce a reading in a service sheet, please remember that the laws of copyright apply and that you may need to obtain permission from the publisher. The Society of Authors provides a guide to permissions on its website: www.societyofauthors.org/publications/quick_guide_permissions.

Choices of songs, hymns and music are very personal. We have given ideas only. Bereaved people will have their own ideas about what music is appropriate to their loved one and to them. There will be songs and hymns that are firm favourites, and pieces of music that evoke special memories of the person who has died. There are no rules – it is good to try to accommodate people's wishes if at all possible. The songs and hymns listed may well be in more than one hymnbook, so do check. Which brings us to copyright permission. Do make sure that you have permission to use the songs you choose. The songs will probably be covered either by your Christian Copyright Licence or by Calamus (administered by Decani Music). Calamus also look after copyright permission for the Taizé Community.

As well as classical music, chants from the Taizé Community, songs from the Iona Community, music composed by Margaret Rizza or Keith Duke or Secret Garden all include gentle and beautiful pieces that are suitable for a funeral or thanksgiving setting and are easy to obtain. Some worship songs can be very moving at a funeral, such as *Lord, I come to you (The power of your love)* by Geoff Bullock. And of course there is much, much more.

We would particularly like to thank two people for sharing their creativity with us. David Davies, Diocesan Music Adviser, Sub-organist and Director of the girl choristers at Guildford Cathedral, has composed the music for three songs in this book. Ann Lewin, author and poet, has generously allowed us to use some of her words.

The Bible readings that we have quoted come from the New International Bible and the New Revised Standard Version.

The aim of this resource book is to make life as easy as possible for the person planning a service, so a CD containing all the material in the book is included with it. We hope the CD will enable the user to download a service, remove anything they do not want, add their own words, or choose some from other parts of the book which they can cut and paste, and so make the service their own. Once the service is personalized all they have to do is print it off. Also on the CD are the illustrations. These are included so that they, too, can be downloaded and personalized. This will work particularly well with the front of service sheets and memorial cards where names of the deceased can be added. Some of the services include illustrations as part of the service sheet. These are also available when printing off the sheet.

Jan Brind and
Tessa Wilkinson

PART ONE: PREPARATION

CREATING A USEFUL FOLDER

If you are a priest or minister reading this, remember that you may have planned, and conducted, many funerals or thanksgivings, whereas the people you are going to see may never have been to any, let alone been involved in planning one. Because of this you may be seen as the 'expert'. They may feel very unsure as to what to suggest or even how much input they can have. One of the first things you can do to help them is to provide a folder of resources. Give them the folder some time before your visit so they can go through it in their own time. They may well know of something they would like, but not know what it is. 'You know the poem they read at the Queen Mother's funeral?', or 'That hymn that Cat Stevens sang'. If families have time to think what they want, then the time you spend with them will be much easier, and they may feel more relaxed, and able to say what they would like.

The folder

This is a 'living' folder that will frequently be added to and revised. Gather material from every source that you have available. Use plastic pockets in the folder, putting several photocopies of each resource in each pocket. Those planning the service can then take out what they think they might use and share these with other members of their families, and you can take the folder home again.

Sample orders of service

Seeing what others have chosen can be a helpful way of starting to think about a funeral.

Readings

There are many websites which have readings for funerals and thanksgivings. There are many books. You can choose Bible readings, secular readings, poems and a selection of reflections. Full lists and selections of readings can be found in Part Five of this book.

Hymns, songs and music

Put the words of a selection of favourite hymns and songs in this section – but also mention that there are countless others just as suitable. You can also provide a selection of CDs to listen to. Once people realize what is possible, and how flexible you can be, they may feel able to suggest music that speaks particularly of the person who has died. By showing them what is possible you empower them to create the right 'Goodbye' for their loved one. Suggestions can also include contemporary, jazz and classical pieces. One family had a recording of bird song to play during the service. This had been a great passion of the man who had died.

Actions

Throughout the book we have suggested many 'symbolic' actions that can be used in a service – you can include some of these ideas in the file along with ideas of your own.

A note on flowers

Even if the family has requested 'No flowers' in the funeral announcement they may want to put something in the church themselves or talk to the church flower arrangers. Flowers are often wanted for a memorial or thanksgiving service – using the church flower arrangers can be a way for the local church community to be involved.

A sample prayer card

Many people like to put small cards in the church for people to sign. Then the family will know who has been there. It is sometimes hard to remember after the event. Instead of this, some people put a book at the church door. People can write short signed messages for the family. Canterbury Press produce funeral prayer cards to put on seats and a Book of Condolence for people to sign.

CHILDREN AND DEATH

There is often much discussion about whether or not children should be involved, and around, when a death has happened, and whether they should attend the funeral. Children are often far more robust than we give them credit for. What they do not need are mysteries. Children will smell out a lie or a half-truth a mile away. It is much better to tell them what has happened, explain what it means, and what will happen next, rather than assume that they are too young to understand, and try to wrap up the truth with half-truths and euphemisms.

Frequently today we want to sanitize death, and not speak the words about death out loud. How often do we hear people saying someone has 'passed away' or that they have 'lost' their mum? As adults we know what the code means, but for children it just causes more confusion. If we lose something we go and find it. What does 'passed away' mean? Passed away where? Listed below are some of the most frequently used euphemisms about death. All should be avoided wherever possible, not just for children, but for adults as well.

She has fallen asleep

This particular expression is guaranteed to stop children going to sleep. If Gran fell asleep and vanished or died, what will happen to me if I go to sleep?

We have lost Gran

This expression is inappropriate and very casual. 'We went out shopping and we lost Gran.' Oh well, never mind, we can always find another one! How much fear must this instil into a child? Imagine being lost knowing that, when your grandmother was 'lost', she was never seen again?

He has passed over

'He passed over.' What did he 'pass over'? We know as adults what we mean by this, but to a child it means nothing.

Jesus loved him, or wanted him, more. He was so good Jesus wanted him

These expressions can really help children turn off from God or Jesus. If God wanted my Dad and took him away from me, why should I have anything to do with God? He might take me away as well. One child became really naughty after his aunt died. Eventually, after months of being very difficult at home and at school, he explained that he was being naughty so that God would not take him away like he had his aunt. He had heard someone say she was such a good person that God had taken her, so he was working hard to be bad to ensure the same thing did not happen to him!

She has gone on a long journey

People come back from long journeys. We take holidays that involve long journeys. This just adds to a child's confusion.

She is resting

Again, this is very likely to stop a child wanting to go to bed and sleep.

Explaining death to children

Sometimes people ask how they should explain death to children. One of the best ways to introduce the subject of death is when there hasn't been one. Obviously this may not always be possible but, if it is, get some of the excellent books that are around about animals dying (like *Badger's Parting Gift* by Susan Varley, or *I'll Always Love You* by Hans Wilhelm) and have them on the bookshelf along with all the other books children have.

Use the death of an animal to explain death

Always take advantage of looking at death if a pet dies or a bird is found in the garden or park. Look at the deadness of the animal and how still it is; it is no longer warm or breathing. Explain about the heart beating during life, and the blood being pumped around the body, and how, when a creature dies, the heart stops working. Encourage the child to feel your heart beating, or their heart beating. Look at how we breathe in and out, and see how the animal is still. Get a small mirror and hold it up to the child's mouth and see how it fogs up from the child's breath. This does not happen when the mirror is held against the dead animal's mouth. By doing this the child is being helped to see what death looks like and feels like in a non-threatening way, helping to remove the mystery and possible fear.

If the child then has someone close to them die it is possible to refer back to the dead animal to remind them what happens when someone or something dies.

Hold a funeral for the animal. Put it in a box, using the real words like 'coffin' and 'burial' and have a small 'service'. It is also possible to talk to children about cremation and burning the body. Children can understand facts given to them in a clear, precise way. Having these conversations may well lead to more questions being asked, so always be prepared to answer them with honesty and truth.

Talking to children about what happens when a person dies

One of the other questions people often ask is what should one tell the children about life after death? Since there are so many different beliefs about what happens after someone has died, the most important thing to impress on adults, when they are talking to children about this subject, is that if they are speaking to their own children they should speak of their beliefs, and if they are speaking to other people's children they should try to ascertain what the child's parents or family believe. What is most difficult for children is when everyone they speak to tells them something different.

In a Western Christian culture many people will speak about the dead person having 'gone to heaven'. As adults we know what this means, but to a child it may sound like going to any other place. 'Daddy has gone to heaven' or 'Daddy has gone to Luton', mean the same. When Daddy went to Luton, he came back. Obviously, when he goes to heaven, he won't come back. So somehow one has to try to convey to the child that this is a place from which Daddy won't come back. The 'for everness' of death is something small children will not understand. Research has shown that the concept of the measurement of time is not fully understood until a child is around 5 or 6 years old, but of course from a very young age a child understands or feels separation, and that is what a newly bereaved younger child is coping with. Be careful not to make heaven sound too wonderful, otherwise children may say they want to die and go to join the person in heaven.

There are some excellent ways of explaining life after death to children using some beautiful imagery – 'the chrysalis and the butterfly' and 'the water bug and dragonfly' are just a couple. The idea of the chrysalis shell, empty and used, ties in very well with the body being a shell which once held the essence of the person. But, once the person dies, that person, or soul, flies free, leaving behind the body now no longer needed. Or the story of the water bug and dragonfly (*Water Bugs and Dragonflies* by Doris Stickney) where the water bug climbs up the water reed stem and turns into a dragonfly, and finds he cannot go back under the water to tell the other water bugs what has happened. Or look at the cycle of a seed, growing, flowering, making seeds and dying, ready to grow again the next season. *Badger's Parting Gift* by Susan Varley looks at how the person, or in this case animal, that has died lives on in the memory of those he loved because of all the things he taught them.

The most important thing is that the child's family say what they feel most comfortable with. Some people will say that when it rains that is when the dead person is crying or taking a shower; others are very matter of fact – the person has died and that is that. Obviously each belief system will have a clear understanding about what happens to us at our deaths. One thing to be careful of is talking about heaven being 'up there'. One child thought he was going to see his dead mother when he went in an aeroplane.

It is not unusual for children to show signs of regression when they have experienced the death of someone close. Bed wetting, thumb sucking and nightmares are all normal, as are lack of concentration, lack of appetite and great lethargy. It is important to remember that children grieve as adults do.

So, finally, tell the truth. Give facts and stick to what you believe. Answer questions when asked, which may happen a lot and be very repetitive, and most important of all be there and offer much love and support.

Should children go to funerals?

This question is often asked before a funeral, and there is no right or wrong answer, but there are things that should be considered beforehand which may help to make the decision.

Going to the funeral allows children to be part of the saying 'Goodbye'

Saying 'Goodbye' is important for children when someone is still alive. When leaving children one usually says, 'I am going now', rather than just vanishing. It is the same when someone has died and is an important part of the journey through grief. This is especially so when someone has died unexpectedly. Just as adults need to say 'Goodbye' at the funeral, so do children. It helps the reality of the death to be seen. Seeing a coffin, though hard, does help to remove any thoughts that the death might not have happened.

Going to the funeral can reduce the fear children might have of something happening that they sense they are being protected from. The unknown may be much more frightening than the reality

What happens at a funeral is something which adults are often frightened of, and it is important that that fear is not put onto children. Both adults and children need information before such a big event. Before going on holiday we tell children what is going to happen, and it should be the same before a funeral. If children know what to expect then they have nothing to fear. If the coffin is going to be in the church before the service take them there to see what it looks like, or take them to the undertakers and show them there. Tell them what will happen through the service, when the coffin will leave, and what will happen to it.

Going to a funeral may reduce fears that children might have from something they may have seen on the television or in a film. Often the reality is much better than the images they may have

We never know what images children may have seen of death and funerals. There are many gruesome images around, so it is important that children are told what is going to happen. If they have seen pictures of skeletons or horror films or video games depicting frightening images of death, they may expect such things to be seen at a funeral. The reality is much gentler and easier to cope with. For example, one child assumed that his brother's body would be taken out of the coffin when it was buried. But with facts given clearly all such fear may be removed, and attending a funeral can become a positive experience.

If children are going to go to a funeral there is no reason why they cannot be involved in planning or participating in what will happen

Being involved in the planning of a funeral helps children feel part of what is happening. If a parent or sibling has died they might help to choose some of the music, or a favourite reading. They might like to do a reading or place some flowers on the coffin or light a candle. Allow them to think with you what would be good and what would work for the whole family.

Often the reason for not wanting children to go to a funeral is because the adults are frightened, so they put their fear onto the children

It is very easy for us to put our fears onto children. Just like children, adults may feel uncertain about going to a funeral. It is important that adults feel free to ask questions and be involved in planning the funeral. Children are often much more able to accept situations than we give them credit for.

Sometimes people worry that children might get upset it they attend a funeral

Getting upset is quite normal at a funeral. So long as children are being well looked after and know what is going to happen, then getting upset is something that they can be helped to cope with, and live through.

Going to a funeral may allow children to see and learn that crying and showing emotion at any age is normal and all right

Adults may fear that the children will be upset if they see adults crying for the first time. This does not have to be a negative experience. Knowing that showing emotion is something that happens to both adults and children is a good thing for children to see. Again, warn them that they may see adults crying. Talk about it and much of the uncertainty will be removed. Funerals are sad events and sad events can make people of any age cry.

Some people feel that children will need looking after when the adults want to concentrate on what is going on and not have to think of the children

If the adults feel that they do not want the responsibility of looking after children during the service, which might be very understandable, then they can ask a friend or family member to take on the specific role of doing this. Place the children somewhere where they can see what is happening and where they can see the important adults in their lives. It might be that at a given moment in the service they join the friend, or go and join their parents. For example, at one funeral the children did not want to walk out behind the coffin, so just before the end of the service they walked out with someone who had been particularly asked to take them out, and they rejoined everyone later. It was because of listening to the children that this was arranged. They wanted to be at the service, but felt that everyone would look at them if they walked out behind the coffin at the end. This way they were not put through that ordeal.

If children go to a funeral they can then talk about it afterwards and revisit the memories

Having shared the funeral with others, children can then be in a position to share the memories with their family and friends. There isn't this mysterious event that is talked about but which they are not part of. There are no secrets, and no 'no go' areas which cannot be spoken about in front of the children. Taking photos of the coffin before the funeral or of the grave afterwards allows the death to be part of everyone's life. These might be included in a book about the person who has died, so it shows their whole journey of life and death, including the funeral. Making a scrapbook for, or with, children, about the person who has died can be very helpful in allowing them to talk about the person who has died and their involvement in their life.

A GLOSSARY OF CHURCHSPEAK

Sometimes the words we use in our church services need explaining to people who are not used to 'churchspeak'. We hope this glossary of some of the words used will help remind those who are planning a church service always to guard against using jargon that not everyone understands.

Affirmation of faith	A statement of belief – in this case what Christians believe
Absolution	Forgiveness, pardon
Blessing of the people	Given by the priest at the end of a service to ask God to watch over those there
Canticle	Psalm
Commendation	Praise, recommendation
Commit	Entrust, place, hand over
Committal	Interment, burial, entombment
Common Worship	The name given to the revision of Church of England services in 2000
Creed	Faith, a statement of belief – in this case what Christians believe
Entrusting	Handing over to the care of God
Eternal	Everlasting, unending, ceaseless, timeless, undying
Eternal presence	God with us at all times
Eternity	Time without end, perpetuity, infinity
Eucharist	Thanksgiving, as in a service of Holy Communion

Gospel	Good News, readings from Matthew, Mark, Luke or John in the New Testament
Grace	Blessing, kindness
Holy Communion	Eucharist, a service where bread and wine (Christ's body and blood) are consecrated and shared in his memory
Intercession	Prayer to God on behalf of the people
Judgement	Ruling, verdict, decision, finding, sentence, conclusion
Keeping vigil	Waiting, watching and praying, usually when we would be asleep
Kyries	Response to a prayer in this Greek form: Kyrie eleison. Christe eleison. Kyrie eleison (Lord, have mercy. Christ, have mercy. Lord, have mercy).
Lectern	A raised desk where the Bible may be read
Litany	A set of prayers with common response by the congregation
Liturgy	Public worship – including words and use of space
Mercy	Compassion, forgiveness, kindness, make whole, pity
Offertory, Offering	Offering of bread and wine at a Eucharist, collection of money during the service
Paschal candle	Large candle lit on Easter Eve as a sign that Christ is risen. It is lit during Eastertide and at baptisms and funerals
Penitence	Repentance, atonement, remorse, sorrow
Prevail	Triumph, win through, succeed, overcome
Pulpit	A raised place in a church from which sermons are delivered
Raise to the fullness of life	A Christian description of life after death
Reconciliation	Making peace with, settlement, understanding, bringing together
Redeemer	Jesus, saviour, liberator, rescuer
Reflections	Memories, thoughts, related words after a reading
Renew the face of the earth	Restore and make new again God's creation in terms of peace and justice

Requiem	A Holy Communion service to give thanks for the life of those who have died – can be part of a funeral service
Resurrection	Rebirth, reappearance, restoration, life after death
Righteous	Good, moral, just, blameless, honourable, honest
Sacrament	The bread and wine at Holy Communion – a visible sign of Christ's body and blood
Salvation	Deliverance, rescue, recovery, escape, release
Saviour	Jesus, redeemer, rescuer, liberator
Sentences	Short verses from scripture at the beginning of a service
Sermon	Address, talk, oration, tribute
Testimony	Statement of faith, proof, evidence, witness
The Collect	A prayer themed for the day which 'collects' all the other prayers together
The Dismissal	The blessing and 'sending out' at the end of a service
The Gathering	The beginning of worship when the assembly or congregation are 'gathered together' for worship
The Lord's Prayer	The prayer Jesus taught us which begins 'Our Father . . .'
The Peace	A time to greet each other and share Christ's peace – particularly before Holy Communion
Trespasses	Sins, wrongdoings, infringements, encroachments
Verily	Truthfully, beyond doubt, really, rightly

PART TWO: FUNERALS

ORDER FOR A FUNERAL SERVICE

Although this book is focusing on 'creative ideas' for pastoral liturgy, as the authors are Anglican we base our ideas on the *Common Worship* order for a funeral. This order allows ministers the freedom to construct a more creative service while still keeping within the approved Church of England pattern. The suggested order comprises:

The Gathering (there must be a welcome and pastoral introduction).
Readings and Sermon (there must be one Bible reading and a sermon).
Prayers.
Commendation and Farewell (authorized words must be used).
The Committal (authorized words must be used).
The Dismissal.

So, within this service order, it is possible to choose a theme, for example 'Chrysalis and Butterfly' or 'Journeying', to run through the liturgy. The theme might relate to the person who has died and be a reflection of the life that he or she has lived. The readings, prayers, music and songs can all be linked to the theme. There are also specific service resources for particular deaths such as the death of a child, or after someone has committed suicide. We have given some suggested themes and ideas for readings, prayers, hymns, songs, music, actions and artwork that might be used with them. Instructions for making the artwork begin on page 167.

We hope that all readers of this book will find resources in it that will fit comfortably within the denominational service pattern that they use. All the authorized Christian funeral rites can be found in *The Funeral Services Book* (Canterbury Press).

RECEIVING THE COFFIN INTO THE CHURCH BEFORE THE FUNERAL

Sometimes it is appropriate to bring the coffin into the church before the funeral. This could be during the daytime or evening before the funeral takes place, or early on the day of the funeral. There are several reasons for choosing to do this:

- If the person who has died was a member of the congregation it brings them into the heart of the place where they have worshipped, and for the final time they can be surrounded by those with whom they have worshipped.
- It marks our journey from baptism, to the place where we received Christ in the bread and wine, and finally where we are received by Christ into his eternal love.
- It can also be very helpful when there are children coming to the funeral. They can be brought into the church before the service to familiarize themselves with what they will see and with what will happen at the funeral. It gives them plenty of time to ask questions.
- It also gives the family some time to 'watch and pray' with the coffin. Often the environment of the church feels more comfortable and familiar than the chapel at the undertakers.
- In some traditions the coffin is open at the funeral and this gives the family and people gathered a quiet time to say their final farewells privately before the funeral takes place.
- If the family wants to screw down the coffin lid themselves this is a good place in which to do it after their final farewells.

If there is to be a brief service during this time the pattern comprises:

The Gathering.
Readings or reflections.
Prayers.
Blessing and Dismissal.
Time for people to stay and reflect in silence.

However, it is a very gentle time that can really take any shape, so can be designed to reflect the needs of the family.

The Gathering

Before the service think carefully about where the family will sit. This can be discussed with the family. They may like to be right up close around the coffin in a circle of chairs, or in the choir stalls, or they may prefer to just sit in the chairs or pews. Remember there will not be many people in the church, so it is important that they sit together.

Some families may decide that they would like the coffin to be in the church when they arrive. If this is the case then everyone can arrive in church and be shown to their places. If the family want to lead or follow the coffin into the church then everyone can gather at the entrance to the church. They might like the coffin to be carried into the church via the font to represent our entering into our relationship with God at our baptism, the start of our Christian journey. The coffin can then be sprinkled with water from the font. There are some excellent prayers given in the *Common Worship* service, or the prayers given below can be used.

As they walk past the font, the family and friends might mark their own foreheads with the water from the font to remind themselves of their journey with Christ from life to death to new life.

The coffin can then be carried to the front of the church and placed in front of the altar, the place where we meet Christ Sunday by Sunday in the bread and the wine – the food for our journey through life, sustaining us until we come to this point of death, where the final journey begins.

It is good to use candles to surround the coffin. The Paschal Candle can stand tall holding the 'Light of Christ', with other unlit candles placed around. Light always overcomes darkness even in the darkest place, and death can be a very dark place for those who mourn. To have candles shining their light into the church representing Christ's Light in the world is a good symbol at this time, and gives a strong message of resurrection hope. This can be reflected in the readings, prayers and music.

If the family have led or followed the coffin into the church, make sure that someone shows them where to go and sit, so there is no confusion about what to do next.

An order of service for receiving a coffin into church

Welcome

If the service begins at the font, the coffin is carried to the font and placed on palls

> We have come here *today/tonight,* and gather around the font, to welcome N back to the place where *his/her* Christian journey began at *his/her* baptism (*if the name of the church where the baptism took place is known, the church's name could be mentioned here*). The start of a journey that lasted X years. Now that *his/her* journey here on earth is ended, we stop for a moment at the font to reflect on the beginning, when *he/she* was welcomed into Christ's family, offered Christ's gift of forgiveness and love, and started *his/her* journey named as one of God's precious children.

The coffin is sprinkled with water from the font, using a sprig of rosemary for remembrance, with the following words

> Through Christ's death and resurrection we are given the message of new hope and new beginnings. As we remember *N's* baptism let us also remember our own. Here we were washed anew in blessed water, we received the Light of Christ, we were given the sign of the cross to defend and protect us and we were welcomed into God's family. As we all gather to say farewell to N let us do so in the sure and certain hope that that love, light and protection given to *him/her* and us at our baptism continues now as we all journey on from here.

> May *he/she* rest in peace surrounded by God's love.

As everyone passes the font they may put water on their heads to remind themselves of their baptism

Everyone leads or follows the coffin to the altar. Here the coffin is placed on the palls

The Paschal candle is lit and these words are said

> Christ, light of the world
> **Shine in our hearts this *day/night*.**
> Christ, light of the world
> **Shine in our darkness this *day/night*.**
> Christ, light of the world
> **Shine!**
> **Amen**

Everyone is invited to light the unlit candles, taking the light from the Paschal Candle

The people go to their seats

Bible Readings

The steadfast love of the LORD never ceases,
his mercies never come to an end;
they are new every morning;
great is your faithfulness.

Lamentations 3.22, 23

Do you not know that all of us who have been baptized into Christ Jesus were baptized into his death? Therefore we have been buried with him by baptism into death, so that, just as Christ was raised from the dead by the glory of the Father, so we too might walk in newness of life.
For if we have been united with him in a death like his, we will certainly be united with him in a resurrection like his.

Romans 6.3–5

For I am convinced that neither death, nor life, nor angels, nor rulers, nor things present, nor things to come, nor powers, nor height, nor depth, nor anything else in all creation, will be able to separate us from the love of God in Christ Jesus our Lord.

Romans 8.38, 39

Other Readings

I dreamt that the time had come
Fernand de Vinck

I dreamt that the time had come to carry back to my Father the
treasures I was sent to gather on earth.
So I held out my chalice to my brother angel to be filled with
the values of my life.
I thought of bright achievement, renown and success,
but they vanished in the emptiness of glamour.
When it was handed back to me,
I found my cup filled to the brim with what I thought were tiny
things,
hardly noticed and long forgotten,
but now, sparkling with the inner light of the love they contained.
Then I walked holding high the grail of my soul
and there was joy in heaven.

Love is this
Anon.

Love is this
That you lived among us these few years
And taught us love.

Love is this
That you died amongst us and helped us
To the source of life.

With all our love
We wish you 'bon voyage'.

Love lives.

I have seen death too often
Anon.

I have seen death too often to believe in death.
It is not an ending, but a withdrawal.
As one who finishes a long journey,
   Stills the motor,
   Turns off the lights,
   Steps from the car,
And walks up the path
To the home that awaits him.

Reflections

Now there is a time for anyone to speak who wants to say something about the person who has died. If there are items that reflect or say something about the person, these can be placed on the coffin. They might include photos, pictures or letters from children, flowers, something that represents their work or hobby, a poem . . .

Prayers

Lord, we hold out to you all those gathered here.
All those who loved N and shared *his/her* journey on earth.
All those who will miss *him/her* as part of their family.
Lord, lighten our darkness.

Use the following if appropriate or write something suitable for the occasion

Lord, we hold out to you all those who nursed and cared for N.
All those who used medical skills to treat *him/her.*
All those who have become 'medical' friends.
Lord, we will miss them.
Lord, lighten our darkness.

Lord, we hold out to you all those who worked with N.
All those colleagues who *he/she* met with *day after day/ for X years* at the *office/factory/name the place of work.*
All those who will see the empty space left by *his/her* death.
All those who will miss *him/her.*
Lord, lighten our darkness.

Lord, we hold out to you all those who went to school with N.
All those who taught *him/her.*
All those who will see *his/her* empty desk.
All those who will miss *him/her* as a friend.
Lord, lighten our darkness.

Lord, at N's baptism we prayed that *he/she* would 'Shine as a light in the world'.
He/she did shine in all our lives and now that light is gone.
We pray that all those times that *he/she* lit up our lives we shall now gather up and take on into all we do in the future.
Lord, lighten our darkness.

Jesus said, 'I am going to prepare a place for you'.
And, 'There are many dwelling places in my Father's house'.
And that we should, 'Set our troubled hearts at rest'.
We pray that as we go from here we can hold onto those words
of comfort, and believe and trust in the resurrection hope.
Lord, lighten our darkness.

There can now be a time of quiet with some suitable music playing

Blessing and Dismissal   May God's love and hope surround you this *day/night*.
Go in peace.
Amen

OR

May God's angels enfold and surround N as we leave *him/her*
here *today/tonight*.
May we be given the strength to cope with tomorrow.
Let us go in peace.
Amen

People can be invited to stay longer for a quiet time to 'watch and pray' with the coffin. These are last precious moments with the body. If it is possible, do not hurry people to leave. If the family are going to close the coffin it can be done now, or after the quiet time

Suggested Music   Gentle Taizé chants are very suitable for this kind of service

The Lord is my light (Taizé)
(*Be Still and Know*)
My peace I leave you
(*Cantate*)
Nada te turbe (Nothing can trouble)
(*Songs from Taizé*)
Jesus remember me
(*Songs from Taizé*)
Our darkness is never darkness
(*Songs from Taizé*)

Or play quiet classical music.

A GREEN FUNERAL

As we think of resources for this book there are many articles and documentaries in newspapers and on television about climate change and the fragility of Earth. We are waking up to the fact that we need to care for the beautiful planet that God has given us. If we do not, the consequences may be catastrophic. Having a 'green' funeral is one last way in which we can lessen the carbon footprint that each one of us makes during our lifetime. These resources may suit someone who has had a special interest and concern for the environment.

We can choose to be buried in a biodegradable coffin – wicker or cardboard – rather than cremated. Burial can be in one of the many 'green sites' around the country. Permission needs to be sought if the burial is not in a cemetery or church graveyard. The Natural Death Centre is a good place in which to start looking. The Natural Death Handbook has a list of 200 green burial sites around the UK and details of eco-coffin suppliers. Use recycled paper to send people details of the funeral and wake. As well as being 'green', promote fair trade by having fairly traded tea, coffee and cakes at the wake. If flowers are going to be used pick them out of gardens or use fair trade flowers available from some supermarkets. Or instead of flowers at the funeral ask people to donate to an eco-friendly charity such as the Woodland Trust. Or ask people to donate an alternative gift through such organizations as Send a Cow or Christian Aid. Or ask everyone to refrain from driving for a day in memory of the person who has died.

The Gathering

Welcome

Introduction   Today we meet to celebrate *N's* life, to give thanks for the gifts which *he/she* shared with us and to say goodbye. *N's* love and concern for the environment is reflected in the words we shall be hearing and speaking.

Opening Responses	God created the heavens and the earth **Thanks be to God!**
	God created the plants and all living creatures **Thanks be to God!**
	From God we come and to God we return **Thanks be to God!**
Bible Readings	**In praise of creation**

Praise the LORD!
Praise the LORD from the heavens;
praise him in the heights!
Praise him, all his angels;
praise him, all his host!
Praise him, sun and moon;
praise him, all you shining stars!
Praise him, you highest heavens,
and you waters above the heavens!
Let them praise the name of the LORD,
for he commanded and they were created.
He established them for ever and ever;
he fixed their bounds, which cannot be passed.
Praise the LORD from the earth,
you sea monsters and all deeps,
fire and hail, snow and frost,
stormy wind fulfilling his command!
Mountains and all hills,
fruit trees and all cedars!
Wild animals and all cattle,
creeping things and flying birds!
Kings of the earth and all peoples,
princes and all rulers of the earth!
Young men and women alike,
old and young together!
Let them praise the name of the LORD,
for his name alone is exalted;
his glory is above earth and heaven.
He has raised up a horn for his people,

praise for all his faithful,
for the people of Israel who are close to him.
Praise the LORD!

Psalm 148

For everything there is a season

There is a time for everything,
and a season for every activity under heaven:
a time to be born and a time to die,
a time to plant and a time to uproot,
a time to kill and a time to heal,
a time to tear down and a time to build,
a time to weep and a time to laugh,
a time to mourn and a time to dance,
a time to scatter stones and a time to gather them,
a time to embrace and a time to refrain,
a time to search and a time to give up,
a time to keep and a time to throw away,
a time to tear and a time to mend,
a time to be silent and a time to speak,
a time to love and a time to hate,
a time for war and a time for peace.

Ecclesiastes 3.1–8

The Beatitudes

Now when he saw the crowds, he went up on a mountainside
and sat down. His disciples came to him, and he began to teach
them, saying:

'Blessed are the poor in spirit,
for theirs is the kingdom of heaven.
Blessed are those who mourn,
for they will be comforted.
Blessed are the meek,
for they will inherit the earth.
Blessed are those who hunger and thirst for righteousness,
for they will be filled.
Blessed are the merciful,
for they will receive mercy.

Blessed are the pure in heart,
for they will see God.
Blessed are the peacemakers,
for they will be called children of God.
Blessed are those who are persecuted for righteousness' sake,
for theirs is the kingdom of heaven.
Blessed are you when people revile you and persecute you and
utter all kinds of evil against you falsely on my account. Rejoice
and be glad, for your reward is great in heaven, for in the same
way they persecuted the prophets who were before you.'

Matthew 5.1–11

Other Readings

We grieve your heart, O God
Jan Brind

We grieve your heart, O God
When we disrespect the world you have given us
So freely
We grieve your heart, O God
When we cover your earth with concrete
Trapping seeds that bring new growth
We grieve your heart, O God
When we tear down your forests
Which anchor the land and shade us
We grieve your heart, O God
When we pollute the water
That should revive and refresh
We grieve your heart, O God
When we fill the air with poisonous fumes
So that your living things suffocate
We grieve your heart, O God
When we dump our unwanted rubbish in your oceans
So that the fish and creatures of the sea are harmed
We grieve your heart, O God
When we see injustice and poverty
And do nothing
We grieve your heart, O God
When we fail to love our brothers and sisters
As you have commanded

We grieve your heart, O God
Oh, how we grieve your heart

Forgive your people, O God, and change us
Soften our hearts
And breathe new life into us
Lead us in your ways of love and truth
That we may care for your creation
And renew the face of the earth

Sermon/Address

Prayers

There is a time for everything,
and a season for every activity under heaven.
**Lord, though we do not always understand why things happen
at certain times,
help us to trust and have faith in you.
May we know the difference between** *chronos* **and** *kairos* **–
***ordered* **time and** *appropriate* **time – that we may not confuse
one with the other.**

There is a time to be born and a time to die.
**Lord, we thank you for N and for the good years that we have
shared together.
Now that N's earthly life is over,
we pray that** *he/she* **is with your saints in heaven,
living in the light and rest that is eternal.**

There is a time to plant and a time to uproot.
**Lord, we pray for your beautiful planet Earth.
May we be better stewards of the planting and uprooting so
that all its bounty may be shared more fairly between rich and
poor nations.**

There is a time to kill and a time to heal,
a time to tear down and a time to build.
**Lord, may we destroy and tear down all that separates us,
and build on those things which draw us together and bring
healing.**

There is a time to weep and a time to laugh,
a time to mourn and a time to dance.

Lord, we pray for all who mourn.
In our grief help us to remember that it is all right for our tears
to turn to laughter
and our mourning to turn into dancing.

There is a time to scatter stones and a time to gather them.
Lord, as your living stones, may we know the right time to set
our loved ones free
and the right time to keep them protected and close.

There is a time to embrace and a time to refrain.
Lord, give us wisdom to know when to offer help to our
neighbour, and when to stand back.

There is a time to search and a time to give up.
Lord, help us to use our time sensibly
and not to seek endlessly after things
which are not ours to have.

There is a time to keep and a time to throw away.
Lord, we clutter our lives with so many inconsequential and
material possessions.
Help us to put away those things which are not needed so that
we may see more clearly the things which are important.

There is a time to tear and a time to mend.
Lord, we are sorry for the people we have hurt and the parts of
your kingdom we have destroyed.
Forgive us and help us to tear down only that which is false and
stand up for what is true and just.

There is a time to be silent and a time to speak.
Lord, help us to know when to stand silently by and when to
reach out with gentle words.

There is a time to love and a time to hate,
a time for war and a time for peace.
Lord, you ask us to love one another
as you have loved us.
May our hatred and our wars only be waged
against poverty and injustice.
May love and peace wash over your people

and may we work to bring in your kingdom here on earth so
that we may one day be found fit to live with your saints in the
light of eternity.
Amen

The Lord's Prayer

Commendation and Farewell

The Committal

The Dismissal	Let us now go from this place. Let us resolve to care for one another and for all God's creation, knowing that it is in God's own good time, and not ours, that we shall be healed and led into the way of peace, and the blessing . . .

Suggested Hymns and Songs	**All things bright and beautiful** (*The Children's Hymn Book*) **Oh Lord my God, when I in awesome wonder** (*Hymns Old and New: One Church, One Faith, One Lord*) **God in his love for us lent us this planet** (*Church Hymnary*) **Jesus put this song** (*Hymns Old and New: One Church, One Faith, One Lord*) **The peace of the earth** (*There is One Among Us*) **Think of a world without any flowers** (*Hymns Old and New: One Church, One Faith, One Lord*) **Touch the earth lightly** (*Church Hymnary*)

Suggested Music	**Shepherd me, O God** CD: *Anthology 2*, Marty Haugen, GIA Publications **The Celtic Spirit** CD: *The Celtic Spirit*, Lion Publishing **To everything there is a season** CD: *Gloria and other sacred music*, John Rutter, Hyperion

Artwork   Decorate an altar frontal with sun, moon and stars and the words 'God created heaven and earth – thanks be to God'. (See 'How to Make a Paper Altar Frontal' on page 170, and template on page 174.)

AFTER A DEATH BY SUICIDE

The sudden, traumatic or violent death of someone is an enormous shock, especially if it is caused by someone committing suicide. The feelings that loved ones and friends have to suddenly confront are in addition to all the more normal and expected grief feelings that are experienced when someone dies from a more natural or expected cause. There are so many 'If onlys' and 'What ifs' to deal with. So many feelings of regret, and of wishing to turn the clock back, and of being unable to do something to prevent what has happened. Feelings of anger and guilt are often present – either directed towards oneself, or directed at someone else, or the person who has committed suicide. Planning a funeral in this case is a particularly sensitive task and requires very careful thought.

The Gathering
Everyone is given a candle and a drip-shield as they arrive

Welcome

Introduction

Opening Responses

The Lord is my light and my salvation;
whom then shall I fear?
The Lord is the strength of my life;
of whom then shall I be afraid?

Hear my voice, O Lord, when I call
have mercy upon me and answer me.

Wait for the Lord;
be strong and he shall comfort your heart;

wait patiently for the Lord.
The Lord is my light and my salvation.

Bible Readings **Do not be afraid**

But now thus says the Lord,
he who created you, O Jacob,
he who formed you, O Israel:
Do not fear, for I have redeemed you;
I have called you by name, you are mine.
When you pass through the waters, I will be with you;
and through the rivers, they shall not overwhelm you;
when you walk through fire you shall not be burned,
and the flame shall not consume you.
For I am the Lord your God,
the Holy One of Israel, your Saviour.
I give Egypt as your ransom,
Ethiopia and Seba in exchange for you.
Because you are precious in my sight,
and honoured, and I love you.

Isaiah 43.1–4

The souls of the righteous

But the souls of the righteous are in the hand of God,
and no torment will ever touch them.
In the eyes of the foolish they seemed to have died,
and their departure was thought to be a disaster,
and their going from us to be their destruction;
but they are at peace.
For though in the sight of others they were punished,
their hope is full of immortality.
Having been disciplined a little, they will receive great good,
because God tested them and found them worthy of himself;
like gold in the furnace he tried them,
and like a sacrificial burnt-offering he accepted them.
In the time of their visitation they will shine forth,
and will run like sparks through the stubble.
They will govern nations and rule over peoples,

and the Lord will reign over them for ever.
Those who trust in him will understand truth,
and the faithful will abide with him in love,
because grace and mercy are upon his holy ones,
and he watches over his elect.

Wisdom of Solomon 3.1–9

Nothing can separate us from the love of God

What, then, shall we say in response to this? If God is for us, who can be against us? He who did not spare his own Son, but gave him up for us all – how will he not also, along with him, graciously give us all things? Who will bring any charge against those whom God has chosen? It is God who justifies. Who is he that condemns? Christ Jesus, who died – more than that, who was raised to life – is at the right hand of God and is also interceding for us. Who shall separate us from the love of Christ? Shall trouble or hardship or persecution or famine or nakedness or danger or sword? . . . No, in all these things we are more than conquerors through him who loved us. For I am convinced that neither death nor life, neither angels nor demons, neither the present nor the future, nor any powers, neither height nor depth, nor anything else in all creation, will be able to separate us from the love of God that is in Christ Jesus our Lord.

Romans 8.31–35, 37–39

Do not be anxious

Let your gentleness be evident to all. The Lord is near. Do not be anxious about anything, but in everything, by prayer and petition, with thanksgiving, present your requests to God. And the peace of God, which transcends all understanding, will guard your hearts and your minds in Christ Jesus.

Philippians 4.5b–7

He will wipe away all tears

Then I saw a new heaven and a new earth; for the first heaven and the first earth had passed away, and the sea was no more.

And I saw the holy city, the new Jerusalem, coming down out of heaven from God, prepared as a bride adorned for her husband. And I heard a loud voice from the throne saying,
'See, the home of God is among mortals.
He will dwell with them;
they will be his peoples,
and God himself will be with them;
he will wipe every tear from their eyes.
Death will be no more;
mourning and crying and pain will be no more,
for the first things have passed away.'
And the one who was seated on the throne said, 'See, I am making all things new.'

Revelation 21.1–5a

Other Readings

When loving someone is not enough
Jan Brind

The phone rings . . . the voice at the other end sounds nervous. There is dreadful news. Shocking news that no one should ever have to give, or receive. *He is dead. He has taken his own life. He was found this afternoon.* In that moment the world is changed and time is suspended. A dreadful silent scream 'No! No! No!' explodes inside me and yet, and yet, with a terrible realisation and certainty, I know it is true. Why didn't he 'phone? He promised he would. Last conversations are remembered and replayed over and over, word for word. What did we miss?

But, sadly, loving someone is not always enough. His pain was such that, for him, dying was an easier option than living. And now we are left, in this place where he is no longer. With the 'If onlys', and the 'What ifs', and a huge sadness and regret that someone we loved and cherished chose not to stay with us, but to go. Such truth is hard to accept. But this we do believe. He is at peace now and his pain is no more. He is with God in a place where all things are made well and where all darkness is overcome. Slowly our pain, too, will be healed, and we will remember him as he was before, embracing life to the full and laughing with the joy of it. And we will smile again at the memory and hold it in our hearts.

From *The Prophet*, Kahlil Gibran

Your pain is the breaking of the shell that encloses your understanding. Even as the stone of the fruit must break, that its heart may stand in the sun, so must you know pain.

St John Chrysostom

He whom we love and lose is no longer where he was before. He is now wherever we are.

From *Revelations of Divine Love*, Julian of Norwich

Because of the tender love which our good Lord feels for all who shall be saved, he supports us willingly and sweetly, meaning this: 'It is true that sin is the cause of all this suffering, but all shall be well, and all shall be well, and all manner of things shall be well.'

Sermon/Address

Prayers

For sunshine and rainbows,
for laughter and tears,
for treasured memories – good and difficult,
and for the gift of N and for all that N meant to us,
we thank you, good Lord.
Lord, have mercy.

For the family of N and those who mourn,
in this time, suspended and unreal,
in our raw emotions and muddled thoughts,
and in our listening and in our words,
be present, good Lord.
Lord, have mercy.

In our searching to make sense of this,
in our regrets and for words unsaid,
in the blame and forgiveness we seek,
and in your compassion,
hear us, good Lord.
Lord, have mercy.

That we may grow in understanding,
that we may trust in the love of God,
that we may believe that all shall be well,
and that we may, at the end, be reunited with the saints in
    heaven,
we pray to you, good Lord.
Lord, have mercy.

From *The Shade of His Hand*
Michael Hollings and Etta Gullick

Lord we cannot understand why N took his own life. You alone know what he suffered. Forgive our lack of understanding, and give him comfort and compassion which we so unthinkingly failed to give. Lord, we pray that he may rest in peace with you in the warmth of your love; and, Lord, give support to his family and those close to him through your healing and redeeming love which you showed us in your Son.
Amen

The Lord's Prayer

A taper is lit from the Paschal Candle and the light is spread to all the people present – the people are then invited to keep a short time of silence when they can offer painful feelings and thoughts to God in the silence of their hearts

Responses   **The Lord is my light and my salvation;
whom then shall I fear?**

Wait for the Lord;
be strong and he shall comfort your heart;
wait patiently for the Lord.

**The Lord is my light and my salvation.
Thanks be to God.**

Commendation and Farewell

The candles remain lit during the Commendation and Farewell and are then extinguished – they can be taken home and lit at difficult times

The Committal

The Dismissal	May the light of Christ shine in our darkness, may the love of Christ comfort and heal us, may the hope of Christ fill us with courage now and in the difficult days ahead, and may the blessing . . .
Suggested Hymns and Songs	**Dear Lord and Father of mankind** (*Hymns Old and New – New Anglican Edition*) **Do not be afraid** (*Be Still and Know*) **Go, silent friend** (*When Grief is Raw*) **God to enfold you** (*Iona Abbey Music Book*) **Going home** (*Be Still and Know*) **Jesus, remember me** (*Songs from Taizé*) **Kindle a flame** (*Celtic Hymn Book*) **Kyrie (Haugen)** (*Cantate*) **My peace I leave you** (*Cantate*) **Nothing can trouble** (Nada te turbe) (*Songs from Taizé*) **O Christ, you wept** (*When Grief is Raw*) **O God, why are you silent** (*Turn My Heart*) **The Lord's my shepherd** (*Hymns Old and New: One Church, One Faith, One Lord*) **There's a wideness in God's mercy** (*Complete Anglican Hymns Old and New*) **We cannot measure how you heal** (*When Grief is Raw*) **Within our darkest night** (*Songs from Taizé*)

Suggested Music	**The Lord bless you and keep you** CD: *Gloria: The Sacred Music of John Rutter*, John Rutter, Collegium Records
	Adagio for strings Samuel Barber
	Lord our God, receive your servant CD: *The Last Journey*, The Cathedral Singers, GIA Publications
	Fields of gold CD: *Songbird*, Eva Cassidy, Blix Street Records
	The Lord is my light and my salvation CD: *Light in Our Darkness*, Margaret Rizza, Kevin Mayhew
	Christ as a light (Prayer of St Patrick) CD: *Celtic Daily Prayer from the Northumbria Community*, Northumbria Community Trust Ltd
	Healer of our every ill CD: *Anthology 2,* Marty Haugen, GIA Publications
	Come to me CD: *Heartcry: Celtic Roots and Rhythms*, Nick and Anita Haig, ICC
Action	Candles and drip shields for everyone
Artwork	Decorate an altar frontal with the words 'May the Light of Christ shine in our darkness'. (See 'How to Make a Paper Altar Frontal' on page 170, and template on page 175.)

AFTER A STILLBIRTH

The death of a child at birth is one of such mixed emotions. A new baby is expected, a dead baby is born. A new life is anticipated but is not delivered. It should be a time of great joy and becomes a time for great sadness. Because of this it has become increasingly recognized that it is very important for those involved to have the opportunity to mark the life and death of their baby, and give thanks for the baby's brief life in the mother's womb. It is also important for the mother and father to mark the fact that they are parents, even though the baby is no longer there. If a child is born near to term, or at full term, most hospitals today will allow the parents, if they want to, to spend time with their baby. Photographs and hand and foot prints will be taken as keepsakes and to help the family have 'proof' of their child's brief life. This will be the only time after birth that the parents will have with their child, so it is very important that the time is a positive and helpful experience if the parents decide that they want a funeral or cremation and it is important that as much time is taken with the planning of this as would be taken with the planning for someone who has lived longer. Many parents will name their child and it is important that the name should be used during the service.

The Gathering

Welcome
We come here today to give thanks for the life of N. Sadly *his/her* life was all too brief, but that makes no difference to us or to God. N was your precious child and God's precious child. So we shall give thanks for N's brief life, we shall hold out to God our sense of loss and confusion, our sense of anger and disappointment, and we shall spend time showing our love and concern for each other and ask for God's healing light to shine upon us and help us to find peace.

Introduction

Opening Responses	Lord, we feel so lost and overwhelmed. **Lord, hear us in our pain and confusion.**

Lord, our arms are empty.
Lord, hear us in our pain and confusion.

Lord, we had such hopes and expectations.
Lord, hear us in our pain and confusion.

N was both our precious child and your precious child, Lord, and *he/she* has died.
Lord, hear us in our pain and confusion.

Bible Readings

Jesus shows his love for children

People were bringing little children to him in order that he might touch them; and the disciples spoke sternly to them. But when Jesus saw this, he was indignant and said to them, 'Let the little children come to me; do not stop them; for it is to such as these that the kingdom of God belongs. Truly I tell you, whoever does not receive the kingdom of God as a little child will never enter it.' And he took them up in his arms, laid his hands on them, and blessed them.

Mark 10.13–16

Nothing can separate us from the love of God

For I am convinced that neither death, nor life, nor angels, nor rulers, nor things present, nor things to come, nor powers, nor height, nor depth, nor anything else in all creation, will be able to separate us from the love of God in Christ Jesus our Lord.

Romans 8. 38–39

Other Readings

A mother's lament
Tessa Wilkinson

I knew you every day as you grew
I felt your first movements as you stretched your growing
    limbs
You were cocooned in that safe warm world within me
protected and sheltered from the outside world
I met you on the scans and marvelled at your creation
I watched your life-giving heart beat

synchronised with mine
Now you are gone
No cries at birth, no phone calls of joy
Just stillness and silence
Your beautiful eyes never to open to look into mine
Your limbs still and lifeless as you enter this outside world
Your heart never to beat again
Your tiny fingers never to cling on
How I yearn to hold you in my arms
To fill the void, the emptiness
You are our child and we love you
Nothing can ever take that from us
We shall always remember you
Our *first/second* . . . precious child

Grief
Anon.

Grief is not for ever, but love is.

Love
Tessa Wilkinson

You were conceived in love
Grew surrounded by our love
Died enfolded by love
Love never dies.

The end of our future
Tessa Wilkinson

When an adult dies it feels like the end of our past
But when a child dies it feels like the end of our future.

Tree of Life
Eavan Boland
(Available to view on the internet, see page x.)

We Trust
Anon.

We trust that beyond absence there is a presence
That beyond the pain there can be healing
That beyond the brokenness there can be wholeness
That beyond the anger there may be peace
That beyond the hurting there may be forgiveness
That beyond the silence there may be the word
That beyond the word there may be understanding
That through understanding there is love.

Sermon/Address

Prayers

Thanksgiving for the baby that has died
The time with N after *he/she* was born was so short, but that in no way diminishes how precious *he/she* is to us and to God. For the past nine months *he/she* had grown and moved, and had taken on an identity as part of the N family. So we turn to God in all our pain and confusion and ask *him/her* to welcome N home to rest in *his/her* loving arms.

Lord, we feel emptiness and sorrow,
Let us know and feel your love.

Prayer for those who mourn
Lord, as the waves of grief wash over N and N as they look into the empty cot, into an empty void, and as they have to answer questions about where their baby is, give them the knowledge of your love for them, and your hope, and your comfort.
We pray they will be surrounded by a loving family and many friends as they journey on together.

Lord, we feel emptiness and sorrow,
Let us know and feel your love.

Prayer of grandparents
Lord, we hold out to you all N's grandparents, as they grieve for their grandchild.
All their hopes and expectations for the future seem to have gone. The pain they feel for themselves is mingled with the pain they

feel for their own child, as they watch and wish they could take that pain away, but know they cannot.

Lord, we feel emptiness and sorrow,
Let us know and feel your love.

Prayer for healing and peace
Lord, we hold out to you all who have gathered here today.
May this time of grief and mourning lead to a time of healing and peace.
May those who have suffered such deep loss know the comfort of friendship and love.
May they be strong for each other and together go forward knowing they are loved by God at all times.

Lord, we feel emptiness and sorrow,
Let us know and feel your love.

The Lord's Prayer

Commendation and Farewell

The Committal

The Dismissal   Let us go from this place in faith and in hope,
knowing we are not alone,
blessed by having shared this time together.

May God's blessing be upon us in times of sadness,
may God's blessing be upon us in times of joy,
may we be aware of God's love in all we do and say.
The blessing of God . . .

Suggested Hymns and Songs   **A cradling song**
(*When Grief is Raw*)
Christ's is the world (A touching place)
(*When Grief is Raw*)
God to enfold you
(*Iona Abbey Music Book*)
Let there be love
(*Hymns Old and New – New Anglican Edition*)

Lord, we pray be near us
(*See 'Music Supplement' on page 240*)
Kindle a flame
(*Celtic Hymn Book*)

Suggested Music   **God's eye is on the sparrow**
CD: *God's Eye is on the Sparrow*, Bob Hurd and Anawim, OCP Publications

Song for Kim
CD: *Heartcry: Celtic Roots and Rhythms*, Nick and Anita Haig, ICC

A cradling song
CD: *I Will Not Sing Alone*, The Wild Goose Collective and Macappella, Wild Goose Publications

Tears in heaven
CD: *Clapton Chronicles*, Eric Clapton, Reprise Records

A Gaelic blessing
CD: *Gloria: The Sacred Music of John Rutter*, John Rutter, Collegium Records

CHRYSALIS AND BUTTERFLY

This may be especially suitable for a child's funeral. The chrysalis looks so empty, dead. It is hard to believe that anything could happen to it to improve on its state of stillness. However could something alive appear from such a dead-looking object? But it does. Something beautiful and very alive appears – a butterfly. This is such a wonderful image to use after someone, especially a child, has died. Their body is dead, but from it comes new life, freed from the constraints of an earthly body, now transformed into a free spirit, changed and beautiful. When Jesus was crucified and buried in the tomb the disciples thought he was dead and it was all over, but they soon discovered that death was not the end of the story, just a continuing of the journey from life to death to new life.

The Gathering

On arrival everyone is given a brightly coloured butterfly wrapped up in a piece of plain paper, and a pen

Welcome

Introduction

In the introduction explain how the butterflies will be unwrapped and used

Opening Responses	From egg to caterpillar, **From conception to birth.**
	From caterpillar to chrysalis, **From life to death.**
	From chrysalis to butterfly, **From death to resurrection.**

From darkness, sadness and despair,
To light, hope and healing love.

Bible Readings

Jesus is not in the tomb

When the Sabbath was over, Mary Magdalene, Mary the mother of James, and Salome bought spices so that they might go to anoint Jesus' body. Very early on the first day of the week, just after sunrise, they were on their way to the tomb and they asked each other, 'Who will roll the stone away from the entrance of the tomb?' But when they looked up, they saw that the stone, which was very large, had been rolled away. As they entered the tomb, they saw a young man dressed in a white robe sitting on the right side, and they were alarmed. 'Don't be alarmed,' he said. 'You are looking for Jesus the Nazarene, who was crucified. He has risen! He is not here. See the place where they laid him.'

Mark 16.1–6

Jesus is not in the tomb

On the first day of the week, very early in the morning, the women took the spices they had prepared and went to the tomb. They found the stone rolled away from the tomb, but when they entered, they did not find the body of the Lord Jesus. While they were wondering about this, suddenly two men in clothes that gleamed like lightning stood beside them. In their fright the women bowed down with their faces to the ground, but the men said to them, 'Why do you look for the living among the dead? He is not here; he has risen!'

Luke 24.1–6

There will be no more night

There will be no more night. They will not need the light of a lamp or the light of the sun, for the Lord God will give them light. And they will reign for ever and ever.

Revelation 22.5

Other Readings

So dead and yet so alive
Tessa Wilkinson

It looked dead, hanging upside down on the underside of the
leaf
Motionless, a small sealed-up grey tomb
Seemingly doing nothing but just being there
Being there, doing nothing
Dead
But . . .
Gradually, gradually, something stirred
Was it movement?
How could it be when it looked so still and dead?
Then the grey tomb started to split
Little by little something began to emerge
Movement, struggle
Transforming death to life
To freedom, to beauty
To a butterfly.

A butterfly
Anon.

A butterfly lights beside us like a sunbeam. And for a brief
moment its glory and beauty belong to our world. But then it
flies on again, and though we wish it could have stayed, we feel
so lucky to have seen it.

The Very Hungry Caterpillar
Eric Carle – Puffin Books (published 2002)

Sermon/Address
*Everyone is invited to release their butterfly and write a message of hope and love
in the white space. The butterflies can be collected in a basket, or stuck on the
coffin, or placed on the altar, hung on a 'tree', or taken home*

Prayers

When our hearts seem cold and still like the chrysalis frozen for
ever in grief.
When we feel dead inside and don't want to go on,
Lord, bring us friendship and love.

When what has happened overwhelms us
and there seems no way of escape,
and to struggle to break free feels too great an effort,
Lord, bring us friendship and love.

When the days warm up and the grief melts a little and there is
a glimmer of hope for healing.
When we feel freed from the burden of sadness
even if it is only for a while,
**Let us rejoice and know that it is all right to laugh again and
to fly free.**

**May we always remember N with love and joy and thank God
for the blessing of having known *him/her* and loved *him/her*.
Amen**

Thanksgiving for the life of the departed
We come together today to give thanks for the life of
N and for *his/her* life among us.
We all hold different memories of *him/her*.
Let us pause for a moment and bring some of those memories
to mind . . . memories of laughter, of sadness, of joy, of hugs
and kisses.
*(Add memories particular to the child. These can be read out
by different voices seated in different parts of the building, or
by one voice. Keep them short and simple)*
We thank you, God, for all these memories and for the way N
enriched our lives.

As we feel the sadness and the stillness of the chrysalis,
**Help us also to remember the hope of the resurrection
butterfly.**

Prayer for those who mourn
The sadness we feel today feels so overwhelming.
God, you know what it is like to have a precious child
die. You want more than anything that we should feel
your love – you, the God who shares our pain and
loss, our sadness and despair. May all who grieve be aware of
your presence. May they be surrounded by their family and
friends, holding them in love, as you hold us all in your love.

As we feel the sadness and the stillness of the chrysalis,
Help us also to remember the hope of the resurrection butterfly.

Prayers of penitence

Lord, we ask forgiveness for the many things we have done which have not pleased you. Forgive us for the
times when we have been short tempered, impatient
and unloving. We know we get it wrong so often, but
we also know that you will always forgive us and
welcome us to start afresh.

As we feel the sadness and the stillness of the chrysalis,
Help us also to remember the hope of the resurrection butterfly.

The Lord's Prayer

Commendation and Farewell

The Committal

The Dismissal

May God who loves us all
Bless us.
May Jesus who died for us
Bless us.
May the Spirit who stirs hope within us
Bless us.
And may the blessing . . .

OR

May you know that God's love surrounds you wherever you
go.
May you know that you are loved and upheld by all those who
walk with you.
May you find healing and peace in the months and years to
come.
Go out from here blessed by God's love.
Thanks be to God.

OR

When the days are empty and sad,

May we know God is with us.

When the nights are long and dark,
May we know God is with us.

When despair seems overwhelming,
May we know God is with us.

May we all feel the warmth of God's love surrounding us, supporting us and leading us on to a place of rest and peace. **Amen**

Suggested Hymns and Songs

Caterpillar, caterpillar
(*The Children's Hymn Book*)
Father be with her family
(*Children's Praise*)
Father for our friends we pray
(*Children's Praise*)
Father, I place into your hands
(*The Children's Hymn Book*)
Go, silent friend
(*When Grief is Raw*)
Healer of our every ill
(*Laudate*)
If I were a butterfly
(*The Children's Hymn Book*)
Morning has broken
(*The Children's Hymn Book*)
Now the green blade riseth
(*Hymns Old and New – New Anglican Edition*)
Since we are summoned
(*Laudate*)

Suggested Music

Canon in D
Pachelbel

The swan
Saint-Saëns

Morning (Grieg)
CD: *The Most Relaxing Classical Album in the World*, Virgin Music Group

Tears in heaven
CD: *Clapton Chronicles*, Eric Clapton, Reprise Records

Majors for minors
CD: *Majors for Minors: Classical Music Nursery Rhymes*, Newsound 2000

Nursery suite
CD: *Cradle Song*, Julian Lloyd Webber and John Lenehan, Kevin Mayhew

Action   Pens for everyone

Artwork

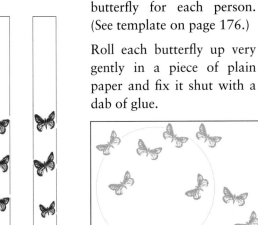

Make a brightly coloured butterfly for each person. (See template on page 176.)

Roll each butterfly up very gently in a piece of plain paper and fix it shut with a dab of glue.

Decorate an altar frontal with butterflies. (See 'How to Make a Paper Altar Frontal' on page 170, and 'How to Decorate an Altar Frontal with Butterflies' on page 177.)

Enlarge the butterfly template. Cut out and hang brightly coloured butterflies from wires strung across the church.

Make a stole and decorate with crosses and butterflies. (See 'How to Make a Stole' on page 178, and 'Butterfly stole' on page 180.)

DESPAIR AND HOPE

Our loved one has died. It could be a close member of our family or a treasured friend. Our lives have changed and, for the time being, we feel numb – our bodies automatically wrapped in layers of protective cotton wool lest we shatter before we have coped with the realities and necessities of death. And then? The terrible pain of grief and disbelief as the reality of loss washes over us in uncontrollable waves and the slow road to healing begins.

Here is a liturgy that attempts to meet the needs and feelings of people at this time. We acknowledge pain and despair, but also hint at the hope and new life that is promised.

The Gathering

Welcome

Introduction

Opening Responses	Jesus said, 'Do not be afraid.' **We put our trust in him.**
	Jesus said, 'I will be with you.' **Though we feel alone now, we know Jesus is near.**
	Jesus said, 'I am the light of the world.' **Whoever follows Jesus will never walk in darkness, but will have the light of life.**
Bible Readings	**My soul longs for you, O God** As a deer longs for flowing streams, so my soul longs for you, O God. My soul thirsts for God, for the living God. When shall I come and behold

the face of God?
My tears have been my food
day and night,
while people say to me continually,
'Where is your God?'

These things I remember,
as I pour out my soul:
how I went with the throng,
and led them in procession to the house of God,
with glad shouts and songs of thanksgiving,
a multitude keeping festival.
Why are you cast down, O my soul,
and why are you disquieted within me?
Hope in God; for I shall again praise him,
my help and my God.

My soul is cast down within me;
therefore I remember you
from the land of Jordan and of Hermon,
from Mount Mizar.
Deep calls to deep
at the thunder of your cataracts;
all your waves and your billows
have gone over me.
By day the LORD commands his steadfast love,
and at night his song is with me,
a prayer to the God of my life.

I say to God, my rock,
'Why have you forgotten me?
Why must I walk about mournfully
because the enemy oppresses me?'
As with a deadly wound in my body,
my adversaries taunt me,
while they say to me continually,
'Where is your God?'

Why are you cast down, O my soul,
and why are you disquieted within me?

Hope in God; for I shall again praise him,
my help and my God.

Psalm 42

For everything there is a season

There is a time for everything,
and a season for every activity under heaven:
a time to be born and a time to die,
a time to plant and a time to uproot,
a time to kill and a time to heal,
a time to tear down and a time to build,
a time to weep and a time to laugh,
a time to mourn and a time to dance,
a time to scatter stones and a time to gather them,
a time to embrace and a time to refrain,
a time to search and a time to give up,
a time to keep and a time to throw away,
a time to tear and a time to mend,
a time to be silent and a time to speak,
a time to love and a time to hate,
a time for war and a time for peace.

Ecclesiastes 3.1–8

The light of the world

When Jesus spoke again to the people, he said, 'I am the light
of the world. Whoever follows me will never walk in darkness,
but will have the light of life.'

John 8.12

Nothing can separate us from the love of God

What, then, shall we say in response to this? If God is for us,
who can be against us? He who did not spare his own Son,
but gave him up for us all— how will he not also, along with
him, graciously give us all things? Who will bring any charge
against those whom God has chosen? It is God who justifies.
Who is he that condemns? Christ Jesus, who died – more than
that, who was raised to life – is at the right hand of God and
is also interceding for us. Who shall separate us from the love

of Christ? Shall trouble or hardship or persecution or famine or nakedness or danger or sword? No, in all these things we are more than conquerors through him who loved us. For I am convinced that neither death nor life, neither angels nor demons, neither the present nor the future, nor any powers, neither height nor depth, nor anything else in all creation, will be able to separate us from the love of God that is in Christ Jesus our Lord.

Romans 8.31–35, 37–39

Other Readings   From *Revelations of Divine Love,* Julian of Norwich

He did not say, 'You shall not be tempest-tossed, you shall not be work-weary, you shall not be discomforted.' But he said 'You shall not be overcome.' God wants us to heed these words so that we shall always be strong in trust, both in sorrow and in joy.

Prayer of St Francis
St Francis of Assisi

Lord, make me an instrument of your peace;
where there is hatred, let me sow love;
when there is injury, pardon;
where there is doubt, faith;
where there is despair, hope;
where there is darkness, light;
and where there is sadness, joy.
Grant that I may not so much seek
to be consoled as to console;
to be understood, as to understand,
to be loved as to love;
for it is in giving that we receive,
it is in pardoning that we are pardoned,
and it is in dying that we are born to eternal life.

I said to the man who stood at the gate of the year
Minnie Louise Haskins
(Available to view on the internet, see page x.)

Footprints
Margaret Fishback Powers
(Available to view on the internet, see page x.)

Bereavement
from *Watching for the Kingfisher*
Ann Lewin

Dark place
Where, vulnerable, alone,
We lick the wounds of loss.
Wise friends say little,
But hold us in their love,
And listen.
There are no guarantees,
Only reports from those
Who've been there,
That there is hope,
And life persists.

Sermon/Address

Prayers

Thanksgiving for the life of the departed
We remember *N* with love and affection and give thanks for *his/her* life. *N's* life has interwoven with ours in so many ways – as *(here name N's relationships to those present)* – and we all have precious memories to cherish. We now entrust *N's* soul to God in the sure and certain knowledge that all will be well.
Compassionate Lord,
We pray to you in hope.

Prayer for those who mourn
Lord, you have said to us, 'Do not be afraid.' When our sadness and grief feels overwhelming give us courage to carry on.
Lord, you have said, 'I will be with you.' We thank you for your presence now. Give us strength to live this day and the difficult days to come.
Lord, you have said, 'I am the light of the world.' Bring us through the darkness into your marvellous light.
Compassionate Lord,
We pray to you in hope.

Prayer of penitence

Lord, as we remember N and the good things we have shared, we also remember the times of regret. We have not always walked in your truth and spoken your peace. In silence we name those things that trouble us, asking forgiveness for past wrongs, so that we may be at peace with N and reconciled to you.

Compassionate Lord,

We pray to you in hope.

Prayer for readiness to live in the light of eternity

Lord, you have said that neither death nor life will separate us from the love of God. From despair bring us to new hope so that we may once more embrace life.

Compassionate Lord,

We pray to you in hope.

The Lord's Prayer

Commendation and Farewell

The Committal

The Dismissal	Compassionate Lord,
	we leave this place trusting that you walk beside us.
	Lead us from despair to hope and from darkness to light.
	And may the blessing . . .
Suggested Hymns and Songs	**As the deer pants for the water**
	(*Laudate*)
	God of the living, in whose eyes
	(*Church Hymnary*)
	God to enfold you
	(*Iona Abbey Music Book*)
	Hear me, dear Lord, in this my time of sorrow
	(*Church Hymnary*)
	Holy God, to you we cry
	(*See 'Music Supplement' on page 242*)
	Lord, we pray be near us
	(*See 'Music Supplement' on page 240*)

My peace I leave you
(*Cantate*)
Nothing can trouble (Nada te turbe)
(*Songs from Taizé*)
Now the green blade riseth
(*Hymns Old and New – New Anglican Edition*)
The Lord's my shepherd
(*Hymns Old and New: One Church, One Faith, One Lord*)
There's a wideness in God's mercy
(*Complete Anglican Hymns Old and New*)
We cannot measure how you heal
(*When Grief is Raw*)
We walk by faith
(*Be Still and Know*)
Within our darkest night
(*Songs from Taizé*)

Suggested Music   Jesus, remember me
CD: *Laudate Omnes Gentes*, Taizé Community, Taizé Community

As the deer longs
CD: *God's Eye is on the Sparrow*, Bob Hurd and Anawim, OCP Publications

Eye has not seen
CD: *Anthology 1*, Marty Haugen, GIA Publications

Neither death nor life
CD: *Gift of God*, Marty Haugen, GIA Publications

Kyrie
CD: *The Armed Man: A Mass for Peace*, Karl Jenkins, Virgin Records

In God alone
CD: *Light in Our Darkness*, Margaret Rizza, Kevin Mayhew

Down ampney
CD: *Sanctuary*, Christian Forshaw, Quartz Music

Artwork   Make an altar frontal and decorate it with footprints and the words 'I love you and I would never leave you' or 'God loves you' or other suitable words. (See 'How to Make a Paper Altar Frontal' on page 170, and footprint template on page 182.)

FOR A BABY OR YOUNG CHILD

The death of a young child is so hard for all to bear. In this funeral service the theme is of a life cut off before it has really started, as would be seen in a beautiful flower in bud which never opens; it had the potential to become a beautiful flower, but never had the chance to open up and be seen in all its glory. That doesn't take away the beauty of the bud, which has shape and colour and smell, but it will never be seen as a flower fully open. It is complete in itself. It is a flower, admired as a bud, as something perfect. But not the whole of the flower's story or journey has happened. So it is with a young child's death. The child is there, complete in itself at that age. But without death there would be much more to come. The sense of not knowing what the child's story or journey would have been is one of the greatest losses when a child dies.

The Gathering

Welcome

Introduction

Opening Responses	A precious child has been born, **A precious child has died.**
	The hope of a new life was there, **The hope of a new life is gone.**
	God, reach out and hold us all in our pain and sadness, **Hold us, Lord, in our sadness.**
	Let us thank God for *N*'s life, **Thank you, Lord.**

Bible Readings   ### God will never forget you

But Zion said, 'The LORD has forsaken me, the Lord has forgotten me. Can a mother forget the baby at her breast and have no compassion on the child she has borne? Though she may forget, I will not forget you! See, I have engraved you on the palms of my hands; your walls are ever before me.'

Isaiah 49.14–16

Becoming like children

At that time the disciples came to Jesus and asked, 'Who is the greatest in the kingdom of heaven?' He called a child, whom he put among them, and said, 'Truly I tell you, unless you change and become like children, you will never enter the kingdom of heaven. Whoever becomes humble like this child is the greatest in the kingdom of heaven. Whoever welcomes one such child in my name welcomes me.'

Matthew 18.1–5

Jesus took children in his arms and blessed them

People were bringing little children to Jesus to have him touch them, but the disciples rebuked them. When Jesus saw this, he was indignant. He said to them, 'Let the little children come to me, and do not hinder them, for the kingdom of God belongs to such as these. I tell you the truth, anyone who will not receive the kingdom of God like a little child will never enter it.' And he took the children in his arms, put his hands on them and blessed them.

Mark 10.13–16

Other Readings   ### A flower bud
Tessa Wilkinson

A flower bud, holding so much beauty and expectation
Perfect in shape and colour and size
But sometimes it never opens.
So like a young child who dies
So beautiful in shape and form

Holding so many expectations for a future journey shared
    together
But it is a journey never to be taken
Never known
A journey which is cut off short and unfinished
A bud which never opened

Henry's funeral
Tessa Wilkinson

When I saw the tiny coffin arrive it took my breath away. Coffins
should be large and hold adults, and be carried by six strong
men on their shoulders. Seeing that tiny shoebox-sized coffin
being carried by one person was one of the most heartbreaking
things I have ever seen.

The end
Tessa Wilkinson

When an adult dies, it feels like the end of our past
But when a child dies it feels like the end of our future

Comparisons
R.S. Thomas
(Available to view on the internet, see page x.)

Epitaph upon a child that died
Robert Herrick

Here she lies, a pretty bud,
Lately made of flesh and blood:
Who as soon fell fast asleep
As her little eyes did peep.
Give her strewings, but not stir
The earth that lightly covers her.

Light (For Ciaran)
Hugh O'Donnell in *Do Not Go Gentle*, edited by Neil Astley

Peace my heart
Rabindranath Tagore
(Available to view on the internet, see page x.)

Sermon/Address

Prayers

Arms have nothing to hold,
memories of smells and sounds are fading.
O Lord, be with all who despair and grieve.

The cot is empty,
the lullaby plays to a vacant space.
O Lord, be with all who despair and grieve.

The ache inside is overwhelming,
the truth of what has happened cannot be faced.
O Lord, be with all who despair and grieve.

There seem no answers to 'Why'?
just a void of silence.
O Lord, be with all who despair and grieve.

Wrap them in your loving embrace,
send people to walk this hard road with them,
and in time bring them to a place of peace.
Amen

People say
Each section of this prayer can be said by a different voice
representing the person speaking

A voice to represent a mother

People say:
'Never mind', you can always have another child.
But I do mind, I mind very much. I wanted and loved this child.
And yes, I may have another, but it will never replace N. *He/ she* will always be part of our family, and be included in our number.
Father God, Mother God, we pray for the right words when we want to bring comfort and support, and the sensitivity to say nothing when just being there is enough.

A voice representing a father

People say:
'How is your *wife/partner*? How is she doing?'
When will people realize that it is my baby that has died as well as my *wife's/partner*'s. That I hurt as well, and grieve as well,

and need loving as well?

Father God, Mother God, we pray for the right words when we want to bring comfort and support, and the sensitivity to say nothing when just being there is enough.

A voice representing siblings

People say:
'Why don't you go out and play, whilst the adults have a talk?'
Don't push me out. I need to talk as well. N was my *brother/ sister*, and I feel sad and lost as well.

Father God, Mother God, we pray for the right words when we want to bring comfort and support, and the sensitivity to say nothing when just being there is enough.

Several voices together

People say:
Nothing, but cross the road and walk the other way, because they don't know what to say.

Father God, Mother God, we pray for the right words when we want to bring comfort and support, and the sensitivity to say nothing when just being there is enough.

Several voices together

Finding the right words at the right time is so hard when someone is hurting so much.

Father God, Mother God, we pray for the right words when we want to bring comfort and support, and the sensitivity to say nothing when just being there is enough. Amen

Thanksgiving for the life of the departed
Lord, N was born and died so quickly, like a flower that buds but never opens.
We thank you for *N's* life.
We thank you for the brief time *he/she* was with us.
We thank you for the joy *he/she* brought.
May *he/she* rest in peace.
Lord, bring us comfort in dark times,
and your joy in the morning.

Prayer for those who mourn
Lord, we hold *(parents' names)* to you.
Bring comfort to them in these dark times.
We pray that they will know your loving arms around them
and that they will know support and love through their family

and friends.
We pray that in the dark time of grief they will be able to support each other.
Lord, bring us comfort in dark times,
and your joy in the morning.

Prayers of penitence
Lord, we do not know or understand why such a young child should die when their life has only just begun. Forgive us our times of anger and despair.
Forgive us our sense of uncertainty and bewilderment.
Lord, bring us comfort in dark times,
and your joy in the morning.

Prayer for readiness to live in the light of eternity
Lord, as we live our lives without N, help us to be people of faith and hope – having faith to believe that all shall be well, hope in the joy of your resurrection and ours, and belief that we shall all meet again one day.
Lord, bring us comfort in dark times,
and your joy in the morning.

The Lord's Prayer

Commendation and Farewell

The Committal

The Dismissal   **Celtic blessing**
Anon.

Deep peace of the running wave to you,
Deep peace of the flowing air to you,
Deep peace of the quiet earth to you,
Deep peace of the shining stars to you,
Deep peace of the Son of Peace to you.

May the road rise to meet you;
May the wind be always on your back;
May the sun shine warm upon your face;
May the rain fall softly upon your fields.

Until we meet again,
May God hold you in the hollow of his hand.

Suggested Hymns and Songs

A cradling song
(*When Grief is Raw*)
All things bright and beautiful
(*The Children's Hymn Book*)
Calm me, Lord
(*Be Still and Know*)
In the bulb there is a flower
(*Church Hymnary*)
There is a place
(*When Grief is Raw*)
We cannot care for you the way we wanted
(*When Grief is Raw*)
When Jesus longed for us to know
(*Church Hymnary*)

Suggested Music

There is a place prepared for little children
CD: *The Last Journey*, The Cathedral Singers, GIA Publications

Long, long journey
CD: *Amarantine*, Enya, Warner Music UK

Song for Kim
CD: *Heartcry: Celtic Roots and Rhythms*, Nick and Anita Haig, ICC

A blessing
CD: *Fire of Love*, Margaret Rizza, Kevin Mayhew

Nursery suite
CD: *Cradle Song*, Julian Lloyd Webber and John Lenehan, Kevin Mayhew

Majors for minors
CD: *Majors for Minors: Classical Music Nursery Rhymes*, Newsound 2000

Action   Everyone is given a flower in bud when they arrive; at a chosen time in the service, while gentle music plays, the buds can be placed on the coffin or altar.

Everyone is given a flower in bud when they arrive, which they can place on the grave.

Some time during the service a basket of flowers in bud is passed around and everyone takes one.

Artwork   Decorate the service sheet with a photo of the child and a flower in bud. (See templates on pages 183, 184 and 185.)

JOURNEYING

Many of us see our life as a spiritual 'journey' from birth through death to what lies beyond. This is the journey of the spirit as it grows and learns from life's experiences. Very often it is the painful experiences in particular that have the most influence on our spiritual journeys – and on our lives. The following resources might be appropriate for those planning a funeral service for someone who has been aware of their spiritual journey. The resources could equally appeal to those planning a funeral service for someone who liked to 'journey' in a more literal sense.

The Gathering

Welcome

Introduction

Opening Responses	From conception to birth, through childhood and into adulthood, **God is with us.**
	From middle age and into old age, and then until death, **God is with us.**
	Through death and into new life in this great mystery, **God is with us.**
	In this never-ending journey, a journey from life to death and to life again, **God is always with us.**

Bible Readings   **O Lord, you search me**

O Lord, you have searched me
and you know me.
You know when I sit and when I rise;
you perceive my thoughts from afar.
You discern my going out and my lying down;
you are familiar with all my ways.
Before a word is on my tongue
you know it completely, O Lord.
You hem me in – behind and before;
you have laid your hand upon me.
Such knowledge is too wonderful for me,
too lofty for me to attain.
Where can I go from your Spirit?
Where can I flee from your presence?
If I go up to the heavens, you are there;
if I make my bed in the depths, you are there.
If I rise on the wings of the dawn,
if I settle on the far side of the sea,
even there your hand will guide me,
your right hand will hold me fast.
If I say, 'Surely the darkness will hide me
and the light become night around me,'
even the darkness will not be dark to you;
the night will shine like the day,
for darkness is as light to you.

Psalm 139.1–12

You will find me

'For I know the plans I have for you',
declares the Lord, 'plans to prosper you and not to harm you,
plans to give you hope and a future. Then you will call upon
me and come and pray to me, and I will listen to you. You will
seek me and find me when you seek me with all your heart.'

Jeremiah 29.11–13

Come to me

At that time Jesus said, 'I praise you, Father, Lord of heaven and earth, because you have hidden these things from the wise and learned, and revealed them to little children. Yes, Father, for this was your good pleasure. All things have been committed to me by my Father. No-one knows the Son except the Father, and no-one knows the Father except the Son and those to whom the Son chooses to reveal him. Come to me, all you who are weary and burdened, and I will give you rest. Take my yoke upon you and learn from me, for I am gentle and humble in heart, and you will find rest for your souls. For my yoke is easy and my burden is light.'

Matthew 11.25–30

Other Readings

I have often wondered
Jan Brind

I have often wondered at this great mystery – that I, so small and insignificant, should have caught the attention of God? Strange that, just when I was feeling so empty and alone, God should beckon and say, 'Come to me – I will be with you. We will face this together.' I know now that God was always there, watching. But I was too busy with the humdrum things of life to notice. Oh, the joy of feeling that presence! And to know that God *is* always there – not just in sadness, but in the laughter and colour and busyness of life. Yes, God is always there – in life, and in death. And in the great adventure that is still to come.

An old Gaelic blessing
Anon.

May the road rise to meet you:
May the sun shine always on your face:
May the wind be always at your back:
May the rains fall gently on your fields:
And until we meet again, may God keep you
In the hollow of his hand.

From St Augustine

People travel to wonder at the height of the mountains, at the huge waves of the sea, at the long courses of rivers, at the vast compass of the ocean, at the circular motion of the stars; and they pass by themselves without wondering.

Crossing the bar
Lord Tennyson

Sunset and evening star,
   And one clear call for me!
And may there be no moaning of the bar,
   When I put out to sea.

But such a tide as moving seems asleep,
   Too full for sound and foam,
When that which drew from out the boundless deep
   Turns again home.

Twilight and evening bell,
   And after that the dark!
And may there be no sadness or farewell,
   When I embark;

For tho' from out our bourne of Time and Place
   The flood may bear me far,
I hope to see my Pilot face to face
   When I have crost the bar.

Footprints
Margaret Fishback Powers
(Available to view on the internet, see page x.)

What is dying?
Bishop Brent

A ship sails and I stand watching till she fades on the
   horizon and someone at my side says, 'She is gone'.
Gone where? Gone from my sight, that is all. She is just
   as large now as when I last saw her. Her diminished
   size and total loss from my sight is in me, not in her.
And just at the moment when someone at my side says
   she is gone there are others who are watching her

coming over their horizon and other voices take up a
glad shout, 'There she comes!'
That is what dying is. An horizon and just the limit of
our sight.
Lift us up, Oh Lord, that we may see further.

The Road Not Taken
Robert Frost
(Available to view on the internet, see page x.)

The Last Battle (final paragraph)
C.S. Lewis

Sermon/Address

Prayers

Thanksgiving for the life of the departed
Lord God, we come together today to give thanks for N and
for *his/her* life amongst us. We have been pilgrims together
with N on this journey of life and shared its joys and sorrows.
As family and friends of N we remember *him/her* with love
and affection. Now N has gone ahead of us to be with you in a
place where *he/she* may find rest and a safe haven. Though *his/
her* journey here with us is over, for *him/her* it does continue,
but out of our sight, and we can be sure that *he/she* is being
welcomed by all the saints in your heavenly kingdom.
Lord, in your mercy,
Hear our prayer.

Prayer for those who mourn
Loving God, may we, the family and friends of N, be comforted
in our sorrow. May we have companions to walk with us as we
journey this road of grief.
May the Light of Christ shine in our lives and show us a way
forward through the darkness. And may we walk gently, feeling
our pain, and befriending it, understanding that pain is present
because love was there first.
Lord, in your mercy,
Hear our prayer.

Prayer of penitence

Forgiving God, we are sorry for the times we have behaved badly or spoken unkindly. In a moment of quiet we think of N and speak to *him/her* in the silence of our hearts, saying those things which we would like to say, so that we may be reconciled to *him/her* and be at peace.

Lord, in your mercy,

Hear our prayer.

Prayer for readiness to live in the light of eternity

Lord God, as a shepherd guides sheep to new pasture and keeps them safe, so you walk with us and guide our footsteps as we journey through life. We pray that, as with the saints who have gone before, we may, in our turn, be found ready to join the great host of heaven.

Lord, in your mercy,

Hear our prayer.

The Lord's Prayer

Commendation and Farewell

The Committal

The Dismissal   **May God the Father watch over us,**
May God the Son lead us,
May God the Holy Spirit light our way,
And may the blessing of the Three be always about us as we leave this place and continue our journey.
Amen

Suggested Hymns and Songs   **Abide with me**
(*Hymns Old and New: One Church, One Faith, One Lord*)
All who would valiant be
(*Hymns Old and New: One Church, One Faith, One Lord*)
Go before us
(*Go Before Us*)
Go, silent friend
(*When Grief is Raw*)
God to enfold you
(*Iona Abbey Music Book*)

Going home
(*Be Still and Know*)
I heard the voice of Jesus say
(*Be Still and Know*)
Lord, I come to you (The power of your love)
(*Hymns Old and New: One Church, One Faith, One Lord*)
May you walk with Christ beside you
(*Be Still and Know*)
We walk by faith
(*Be Still and Know*)
Will you come and follow me
(*Iona Abbey Music Book*)

Suggested Music   Long, long journey
CD: *Amarantine*, Enya, Warner Music UK

Nunc dimittis
CD: *Sanctuary*, Christian Forshaw, Quartz Music

May you walk with Christ beside you
CD: *Walk with Christ*, Stephen Dean, OCP Publications

Come to me
CD: *Fountain of Life*, Margaret Rizza, Kevin Mayhew

Go before us
CD: *Go Before Us*, Bernadette Farrell, OCP Publications

Let your restless heart be still
CD: *The Last Journey*, The Cathedral Singers

The last journey (From the falter of breath)
CD: *The Last Journey*, The Cathedral Singers, GIA Publications

Journey prayers
CD: *Take This Moment*, The Cathedral Singers, GIA Publications

Nunc dimittis
CD: *Take This Moment*, The Cathedral Singers, GIA Publications

Action   Place candles in jam-jars, either carefully at floor level at the edges of the central aisle, or on the ends of pews nearest the central aisle, to light the way.

Give everyone a candle and drip-shield. The first candle is lit from the Paschal Candle and the light is then passed around the people while music is played to show that the Light of Christ continues to show us the way.

Artwork   Cut out paper footprints and fix them to the floor leading up the aisle. This might be particularly appropriate if 'Footprints' is being used.

Make an altar frontal and decorate with the words, 'God is with us' or other suitable words. (See 'How to Make a Paper Altar Frontal' on page 170, and template on page 186.)

LOVE

A reading that is chosen frequently at funerals is 1 Corinthians 13.1–13, 'And now faith, hope, and love abide, these three; and the greatest of these is love.' In this reading Paul suggests that without love nothing else matters. Love is patient and kind: not envious or boastful or arrogant or rude, but bears all things and believes all things and rejoices in the truth. Love endures all things and never ends. The reading goes on to suggest that, just as we pass from childhood to adulthood and change accordingly, when we die we pass from that which is imperfect to that which is perfect – that there is a new beginning when all things will be made clear. This reading is comforting to those who grieve. The words gather up and describe the feelings we may have for a loved one who has died, and at the same time give hope and reassurance that all will be made well.

The Gathering

Welcome

Introduction

Opening Responses	Jesus said, 'Love one another as I have loved you.' **We are enfolded in the love of Christ.**
	In our sorrow and in our pain, **Jesus is with us and we are not alone.**
	Jesus said, 'Remain in my love.' **We will seek comfort in the love of Christ.**
Bible Readings	**The LORD is my light and my salvation**
	The LORD is my light and my salvation; whom shall I fear? The LORD is the stronghold of my life; of whom shall I be afraid?

When evildoers assail me
to devour my flesh –
my adversaries and foes –
they shall stumble and fall.

Though an army encamp against me,
my heart shall not fear;
though war rise up against me,
yet I will be confident.

One thing I asked of the LORD,
that will I seek after:
to live in the house of the LORD
all the days of my life,
to behold the beauty of the LORD,
and to inquire in his temple.

For he will hide me in his shelter
in the day of trouble;
he will conceal me under the cover of his tent;
he will set me high on a rock.

Now my head is lifted up
above my enemies all around me,
and I will offer in his tent
sacrifices with shouts of joy;
I will sing and make melody to the LORD.

Psalm 27.1–6

Many waters cannot quench love

Set me as a seal upon your heart,
as a seal upon your arm;
for love is strong as death,
passion fierce as the grave.
Its flashes are flashes of fire,
a raging flame.
Many waters cannot quench love,
neither can floods drown it.
If one offered for love
all the wealth of one's house,
it would be utterly scorned.

The Song of Solomon 8.6–7

Love one another

As the Father has loved me, so have I loved you. Now remain in my love. If you obey my commands, you will remain in my love, just as I have obeyed my Father's commands and remain in his love. I have told you this so that my joy may be in you and that your joy may be complete. My command is this: Love each other as I have loved you. Greater love has no-one than this, that he lay down his life for his friends. You are my friends if you do what I command. I no longer call you servants, because a servant does not know his master's business. Instead, I have called you friends, for everything that I learned from my Father I have made known to you. You did not choose me, but I chose you and appointed you to go and bear fruit – fruit that will last. Then the Father will give you whatever you ask in my name. This is my command: Love each other.

John 15.9–17

Love

If I speak in the tongues of mortals and of angels, but do not have love, I am a noisy gong or a clanging cymbal. And if I have prophetic powers, and understand all mysteries and all knowledge, and if I have all faith, so as to remove mountains, but do not have love, I am nothing. If I give away all my possessions, and if I hand over my body so that I may boast, but do not have love, I gain nothing.

Love is patient; love is kind; love is not envious or boastful or arrogant or rude. It does not insist on its own way; it is not irritable or resentful; it does not rejoice in wrongdoing, but rejoices in the truth. It bears all things, believes all things, hopes all things, endures all things.

Love never ends. But as for prophecies, they will come to an end; as for tongues, they will cease; as for knowledge, it will come to an end. For we know only in part, and we prophesy only in part; but when the complete comes, the partial will come to an end. When I was a child, I spoke like a child, I thought like a child, I reasoned like a child; when I became an adult, I put an end to childish ways. For now we see in a mirror, dimly, but then we will see face to face. Now I know only in part; then I will know fully, even as I have been fully known. And now faith, hope, and love abide, these three; and the greatest of these is love.

1 Corinthians 13.1–13

Other Readings

Love lingers
Richard Fife
(Available to view on the internet, see page x.)

From **Journey for a Soul**
Anon.

Death is part of the future for everyone. It is the last post of this life and the reveille of the next. Death is the end of our present life, it is the parting from loved ones, it is the setting out into the unknown. We overcome death by accepting it as the will of a loving God, by finding him in it. Death, like birth, is only a transformation, another birth. When we die we shall change our state – that is all. And in faith in God, it is as easy and natural as going to sleep here and waking up there.

From **St Augustine**

In so much as love grows in you so in you beauty grows. For love is the beauty of the soul.

Sermon/Address

A Litany

For N, in thanksgiving for *his/her* life and for the joy of knowing *him/her* in the journey that we have shared together:
In your love, Lord, enfold N.

For all that N meant to us, for *(insert personal and relevant information here)*:
In your love, Lord, enfold N.

For those who mourn N that we may reach out in love to each other and not be afraid to acknowledge our pain and sorrow:
In your love, Lord, comfort us.

For the times when our grief overwhelms us and seems almost too much to bear:

In your love, Lord, comfort us.

For the things we have said and done wrong which we regret and for which we are sorry:
In your love, Lord, forgive us.

For the times we have failed to care for each other:
In your love, Lord, forgive us.

For times when the future seems unclear, that you will bring us to your light:
In your love, Lord, guide us.

For our longing to be a people fit to join your saints in heaven:
In your love, Lord, guide us.

For these our prayers that you will hear us, merciful Lord, and come to our help:
In your love, Lord, comfort us, forgive us, and guide us, that we may be led in the way of your truth and become a people of your kingdom.
Amen

The Lord's Prayer

Commendation and Farewell

The Committal

The Dismissal   Let us go from this place in faith and in hope, and let us love one another as Jesus has loved us.

And the blessing . . .

Suggested Hymns and Songs   **Bless the Lord, my soul**
(Songs from Taizé)
Day is done, but love unfailing
(Be Still and Know)
For all the saints who showed your love
(When Grief is Raw)
Give thanks for those
(Hymns Old and New: One Church, One Faith, One Lord)

Immortal love, for ever full
(*Hymns Old and New: One Church, One Faith, One Lord*)
In heavenly love abiding
(*Hymns Old and New: One Church, One Faith, One Lord*)
In the darkness of the still night
(*Be Still and Know*)
Let there be love
(*Hymns Old and New – New Anglican Edition*)
Lord, the light of your love (Shine, Jesus, shine)
(*The Children's Hymn Book*)
May flights of angels
(*Laudate*)
Song of Farewell
(*Laudate*)
Thanks be to God
(*Hymns Old and New: One Church, One Faith, One Lord*)
There's a wideness in God's mercy
(*Complete Anglican Hymns Old and New*)
Unless a grain of wheat
(*Restless is the Heart*)
Watch, O Lord
(*Turn My Heart*)

Suggested Music   A blessing
CD: *Fire of Love*, Margaret Rizza, Kevin Mayhew

Go, silent friend
CD: *The Last Journey*, The Cathedral Singers, GIA Publications

Gathered in the love of Christ/Canon in D
CD: *The Song and the Silence*, Marty Haugen, GIA Publications

A Gaelic blessing
CD: *Gloria: The Sacred Music of John Rutter*, The Cambridge
Singers, Collegium Records

The Lord is my shepherd
CD: *Gloria: The Sacred Music of John Rutter*, The Cambridge
Singers, Collegium Records

The hand of God shall hold you
CD: *All Are Welcome*, Marty Haugen, GIA Publications

Artwork   Make an altar frontal decorated with the words 'God loves you and would never leave you'. (See 'How to Make a Paper Altar Frontal' on page 170, and template on page 187.)

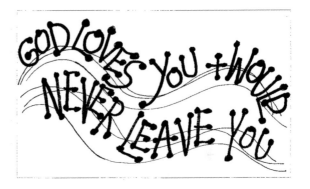

AFTER THE SUDDEN DEATH OF A YOUNG ADULT

Georgia French (14.11.89–24.3.07) radiated energy and love for life. She died during her gap year as the result of an accident. This service is based on the service created by Canon Guy Wilkinson for her funeral and burial, and is reproduced here with permission from her parents. Extracts have been taken from *Common Worship: Services and Prayers for the Church of England* and *Common Worship: Pastoral Services*. Many of the people present at her funeral did not normally attend a church.

Sometimes the words for the funeral service can see very full of 'churchspeak'. This is fine for those who are familiar with that language, but for those who are not, the meaning of what is being said can seem obscure and inaccessible. This service has been compiled to try to address that difficulty.

Welcome	Whether we who are gathered here today have a Christian faith, a faith in this life but not in anything further, or are among those who are unsure about any of this, we nevertheless share in common the real and overwhelming sense of loss at the death of a loved one. We will each have had our own experiences of their life and death, with different memories and different feelings of love, grief and respect. To acknowledge all this together should help us to use this occasion to express our feelings as we say farewell to N. It should help us to acknowledge our loss and our sorrow, and to reflect on our own mortality. Those who mourn need support and consolation and our presence together here today is part of that continuing support.
	Christians believe that every life, including our own, is precious

to God and that there is hope in death as in life. Their hope for a continuing life after life is founded in the understanding and experience of the life, death and resurrection of Jesus Christ. This understanding underlies many of the words used in this service, but, whatever words are used, our common desire is to give thanks for *N's* life, for mutual comfort and for future life.

Introduction

We have come here today
to remember *N*,
to give thanks for *his/her* life;
to commend *him/her* to God;
to commit *his/her* body to be buried,
and to comfort one another in our grief.

Silence

We scarcely know the words to speak,
we scarcely know if they are heard.
When all seems dark, we look for light.
When all is pain, we long for help.
In the silence we wait.

Silence

We grieve for *N* and mourn our loss.
Accept all that was good in *him/her.*
Forgive all that was wrong in *him/her* and in us.
For past joy we give thanks,
in present sorrow we seek courage.
In the silence we wait.*

Bible Reading

The Lord is my shepherd

The Lord is my shepherd;
therefore can I lack nothing.

He makes me lie down in green pastures
and leads me beside still waters.

He shall refresh my soul
and guide me in the paths of righteousness for his name's sake.

---

* Taken from *In Sure and Certain Hope* written and compiled by Paul Sheppy (published by Canterbury Press 2003)

Though I walk through the valley of the shadow of death, I
will fear no evil;
for you are with me; your rod and your staff, they comfort
me.

You spread a table before me in the presence of those who
trouble me;
you have anointed my head with oil and my cup shall be full.

Surely goodness and loving mercy shall follow me all the days
of my life,
and I will dwell in the house of the Lord for ever.

Psalm 23

Other Readings

After Glow
Anon.

I'd like the memory of me
to be a happy one.
I'd like to leave an after glow
of smiles when life is done.
I'd like to leave an echo
whispering softly down the ways,
of happy times and laughing times
and bright and sunny days.
I'd like the tears of those who grieve,
to dry before the sun
of happy memories
that I leave when life is done.

Memories in the Heart
Anon.

Feel no guilt in laughter, she knows how much you care
Feel no sorrow in a smile that she's not here to share
You cannot grieve forever, she would not want you to
She'd hope that you can carry on, the way you always
    do
So talk about the good times and the ways you showed
    you cared

The days you spent together, all the happiness you shared
Let memories surround you
A word someone may say
Will suddenly recapture a time, an hour, a day
That brings her back as clearly as though she were still
   here
And fills you with the feelings that she is always near
For if you keep these moments, you will never be apart
And she will live forever locked safe within your heart.

Prayer of Faith
Anon.

We trust that beyond absence there is a presence.
That beyond the pain there can be healing.
That beyond the brokenness there can be wholeness.
That beyond the anger there may be peace.
That beyond the hurting there may be forgiveness.
That beyond the silence there may be the word.
That beyond the word there may be understanding.
That through understanding there is love.

Sermon/Address

Prayers

God of love, Lord of life,
you have made us to reflect your beauty, truth and light:
we give you thanks for N,
for all that was good in *his/her* life,
and for the memories we treasure today.

You hold out the promise of continuing life.
Remember for good, N, loved by so many
as we also remember *him/her*.
Bring all who have loved or been loved
into the fullness of your future,
where all is healed and death is no more.

Your mighty power can bring joy out of grief
and life out of death.
Look in love on N and on all who mourn.
Give them patient faith in times of darkness.
Strengthen them with an awareness of your love.

When understanding is gone, and confusion overwhelms,
Remember we are not alone.

When nothing makes sense and pain seems all around,
Remember we are not alone.

When life feels fragile and insecure,
Remember we are not alone.

Remember we are all together,
And together we will get through.

Commendation   Let us commend N to God,
and Farewell   who is beyond our understanding
in the hope and expectation that there is more life to come.

The Lord is full of compassion and mercy,
slow to anger and of great goodness.
As a parent is tender towards children,
so is the Lord tender to those that love.
For God knows of what we are made;
God remembers that we are but dust.
Our days are like the grass;
we flourish like a flower of the field;
when the wind goes over it, it is gone
and its place will know it no more.
But the loving kindness of the Lord endures
for ever and ever toward those that love God
and God's care is upon their children's children.

The coffin is placed in the grave and earth or flowers are placed on it

The Committal   We have entrusted N to God's mercy,
and we now commit *his/her* body to the ground:
earth to earth, ashes to ashes, dust to dust:
in sure and certain hope of the resurrection to eternal life
through our Lord Jesus Christ,
who died, was buried and rose again for us
and who can transform our frail bodies.
To him be glory for ever and ever.

The Lord's Prayer Our Father in heaven,
hallowed be your name,
your kingdom come,
your will be done,
on earth as in heaven.
Give us today our daily bread.
Forgive us our sins
as we forgive those who sin against us.
Lead us not into temptation
but deliver us from evil.
For the kingdom, the power,
and the glory are yours
now and for ever.
Amen

Support us, O Lord,
all the day long of this troublous life,
until the shadows lengthen and the evening comes,
the busy world is hushed,
the fever of life is over
and our work is done.
Then, Lord, in your mercy grant us a safe lodging,
a holy rest, and peace at last;
through Christ our Lord.
Amen

The Blessing May God give you
his comfort and his peace,
his light and his joy,
in this world and the next;
and the blessing of God almighty,
the Father, the Son, and the Holy Spirit,
be among you and remain with you always.
Amen

FUNERAL SERVICE AT A CREMATORIUM FOR A NON-CHURCHGOER

A funeral service at a crematorium may follow a service in church, or precede it. Or it may be the only service. A service at a crematorium, where there has been no funeral service in church, and when there is to be no memorial and thanksgiving service afterwards, may be the only time that people gather to say farewell to the person who has died.

Traditionally, cremation services have had to fit into a 'twenty-minute slot'. It is possible to fit the bare outline of the funeral liturgy into twenty minutes – but often not possible to sing a song or hymn or to read more than one reading, and the funeral can feel very rushed. However, some crematoria are now allowing a longer time for each service and, indeed, sometimes it is possible to book two 'slots' next to each other.

After the Committal the coffin may disappear from view – either by sliding away through a door, or behind curtains which slowly close, or by lowering through the floor. This may help some people to say goodbye to the person who has died, but for many others it is distressing. It is perfectly all right to ask for the coffin to stay where it is until the people have left the building.

Here are resources for a liturgy for someone who, although not a regular churchgoer, would nevertheless like a Christian funeral.

The Gathering

Welcome

Introduction

Opening Responses

Though we stray like lost sheep,
You are the Good Shepherd who brings us home.

Though we fail to live in the light of your presence,
You welcome us into your kingdom.

Though our sight is now veiled,
You shall make all things clear.

The Lord is with us here,
Thanks be to God.

Bible Readings

The Lord is my shepherd

The LORD is my shepherd, I shall not be in want.
He makes me lie down in green pastures,
he leads me beside quiet waters,
he restores my soul.
He guides me in paths of righteousness
for his name's sake.
Even though I walk
through the valley of the shadow of death,
I will fear no evil,
for you are with me;
your rod and your staff,
they comfort me.
You prepare a table before me
in the presence of my enemies.
You anoint my head with oil;
my cup overflows.
Surely goodness and love will follow me
all the days of my life,
and I will dwell in the house of the LORD for ever.
Psalm 23

God knows all about me

O LORD, you have searched me
and you know me.
You know when I sit and when I rise;
you perceive my thoughts from afar.
You discern my going out and my lying down;

you are familiar with all my ways.
Before a word is on my tongue
you know it completely, O LORD.
You hem me in – behind and before;
you have laid your hand upon me.
Such knowledge is too wonderful for me,
too lofty for me to attain.
Where can I go from your Spirit?
Where can I flee from your presence?
If I go up to the heavens, you are there;
if I make my bed in the depths, you are there.
If I rise on the wings of the dawn,
if I settle on the far side of the sea,
even there your hand will guide me,
your right hand will hold me fast.
If I say, 'Surely the darkness will hide me
and the light become night around me,'
even the darkness will not be dark to you;
the night will shine like the day,
for darkness is as light to you.

Psalm 139.1–12

I have called you by name

But now thus says the LORD,
he who created you, O Jacob,
he who formed you, O Israel:
Do not fear, for I have redeemed you;
I have called you by name, you are mine.
When you pass through the waters, I will be with you;
and through the rivers, they shall not overwhelm you;
when you walk through fire you shall not be burned,
and the flame shall not consume you.
For I am the LORD your God,
the Holy One of Israel, your Saviour.
I give Egypt as your ransom,
Ethiopia and Seba in exchange for you.
Because you are precious in my sight,
and honoured, and I love you.

Isaiah 43.1–4

Other Readings

The calling
Jan Brind

Though we do not always walk in your Way
Or speak your Truth, or live your risen Life
And though we deny you over and over again
Still, Lord, you call us to be with you

When we think selfishly only of ourselves
And fail to see the needs of our neighbour
Or when we ignore the pain of your world around us
Still, Lord, you call us to be with you

Lord, you know us and call us by our name
And we are precious in your sight
You love us today, tomorrow and for all time
Knowing this – how can we hesitate?

Lord, we come to you with joy in our hearts

Sermon/Address

Prayers

Thanksgiving for the life of the departed
Lord, we thank you for N and for the weaving of *his/her* life within ours. Your Holy Spirit was at work in *him/her* for all of us to see and our lives are the richer for having known *him/her*. Though N would not talk about *his/her* faith it was lived out in all that *he/she* did.
Lord, in your mercy,
Hear our prayer.

Prayer for those who mourn
Lord, we pray for those who mourn N. May *his/her* family and friends draw closer to you and feel your loving and compassionate presence in their lives.
May we remember N with joy in our hearts and know that *he/she* is being welcomed in heaven by you and all your saints who have gone before.
Lord, in your mercy,
Hear our prayer.

Prayer of penitence

Lord, we are sorry and ask your forgiveness for the times we have failed to be your loving disciples. We have not always walked in your Way, or spoken your Truth, or lived the Life you will for us. We are sorry for the times we have strayed from you. In the silence of our hearts we offer to you all that burdens us.

Silence

Lord, in your mercy,

Hear our prayer.

Prayer for readiness to live in the light of eternity

Lord, we pray that we may reflect the light of your love in all that we do as we continue to journey through life, so that, at its end, we may be ready to join with your saints in heaven in the light that is eternal.

Lord, in your mercy,

Hear our prayer.

The Lord's Prayer

Commendation and Farewell

The Committal

The Dismissal	Lord, we say farewell to N and give *him/her* to your safekeeping. We ask you to hold us, and keep us in your love, as we go from this place. And may the blessing . . .
Suggested Hymns and Songs	Abide with me (*Hymns Old and New: One Church, One Faith, One Lord*) **Be still, my soul** (*Be Still and Know*) **Dear Lord and Father of mankind** (*Hymns Old and New – New Anglican Edition*) **Do not be afraid** (*Be Still and Know*) **I heard the voice of Jesus say** (*Be Still and Know*) **O Lord, my God** (*Hymns Old and New: One Church, One Faith, One Lord*)

The Lord's my shepherd
(*Hymns Old and New: One Church, One Faith, One Lord*)
There's a wideness in God's mercy
(*Complete Anglican Hymns Old and New*)
Thine be the glory
(*Hymns Old and New: One Church, One Faith, One Lord*)

Suggested Music   In our tears
CD: *Dreamcatcher*, Secret Garden, Philips

The Lord bless you and keep you
CD: *Gloria: The Sacred Music of John Rutter*, The Cambridge Singers, Collegium Records

Deep peace
CD: *Sacred Pathway*, Keith Duke, Kevin Mayhew

I will arise and go to Jesus
CD: *Haven: Celtic Roots and Rhythms*, Nick and Anita Haig, ICC

Go forth into the world
CD: *Gloria: The Sacred Music of John Rutter*, The Cambridge Singers, Collegium Records

PART THREE: MEMORIAL AND THANKSGIVING SERVICES

ORDER FOR A MEMORIAL AND THANKSGIVING SERVICE

As with the previous section on funerals, the creative ideas here are intended to supplement authorized denominational liturgies. They are based on the *Common Worship* order for a memorial and thanksgiving service. This order allows ministers the freedom to construct a more personal service while still keeping within the approved Church of England pattern. The order comprises:

The Gathering (there must be a welcome and pastoral introduction).
Readings and Sermon (there must be one Bible reading and a Sermon).
Prayers.
Commendation (authorized words must be used).
The Dismissal.

So, within this service order, it is possible to choose a theme, for example 'The Sea' or 'Waterbugs and Dragonflies', to run through the liturgy. The theme might relate to the person who has died and be a reflection of the life that he or she has lived. The readings, prayers, music and songs can all be linked to the theme. There are also specific service resources for particular situations such as following a death from dementia, or after the death of a young person. We have given some suggested themes and ideas for readings, prayers, hymns, songs, music, actions and artwork that might be used with them.

AFTER A DEATH FROM DEMENTIA

At the time of writing this book it is thought that one person in five over the age of 85 is suffering from dementia of one sort or another. Dementia is distressing not only for the person who is ill, but also for family, loved ones and friends. A person affected with dementia not only loses short-term memory and the ability to function independently, but withdraws from reality very slowly, possibly over a period of some years, before dying. Relationships with the people nearest to them are often strained and, in the end, additional help may be needed for both the patient and the carers. Much of the work of grief may have taken place while the person is still alive. Dementia is sometimes called 'the long bereavement'. A memorial and thanksgiving service in this instance can be a chance for people to remember and 're-member' the person who has died – literally to put the person back together again and recall happier times.

The Gathering

Welcome

Introduction

Opening **Responses**	Those who wait on the Lord shall renew their strength, **They shall mount up with wings like eagles,** **they shall run and not be weary,** **they shall walk and not faint.**
	Weeping may linger for the night, **But joy comes with the morning.**

Bible Readings   **Wait patiently for the Lord**

I waited patiently for the LORD;
he turned to me and heard my cry.
He lifted me out of the slimy pit,
out of the mud and mire;
he set my feet on a rock
and gave me a firm place to stand.
He put a new song in my mouth,
a hymn of praise to our God.
Many will see and fear
and put their trust in the LORD.

Psalm 40.1–3a

Depending on others

I tell you the truth, when you were younger you dressed yourself
and went where you wanted; but when you are old you will
stretch out your hands, and someone else will dress you and
lead you where you do not want to go.

John 21.18

Love

If I speak in the tongues of mortals and of angels, but do not
have love, I am a noisy gong or a clanging cymbal. And if I
have prophetic powers, and understand all mysteries and all
knowledge, and if I have all faith, so as to remove mountains,
but do not have love, I am nothing. If I give away all my
possessions, and if I hand over my body so that I may boast,
but do not have love, I gain nothing.

Love is patient; love is kind; love is not envious or boastful
or arrogant or rude. It does not insist on its own way; it is
not irritable or resentful; it does not rejoice in wrongdoing,
but rejoices in the truth. It bears all things, believes all things,
hopes all things, endures all things.

Love never ends. But as for prophecies, they will come to an
end; as for tongues, they will cease; as for knowledge, it will
come to an end. For we know only in part, and we prophesy

only in part; but when the complete comes, the partial will come to an end.

When I was a child, I spoke like a child, I thought like a child, I reasoned like a child; when I became an adult, I put an end to childish ways. For now we see in a mirror, dimly, but then we will see face to face. Now I know only in part; then I will know fully, even as I have been fully known. And now faith, hope, and love abide, these three; and the greatest of these is love.

1 Corinthians 13.1–13

See, I am making all things new

Then I saw a new heaven and a new earth; for the first heaven and the first earth had passed away, and the sea was no more. And I saw the holy city, the new Jerusalem, coming down out of heaven from God, prepared as a bride adorned for her husband. And I heard a loud voice from the throne saying, 'See, the home of God is among mortals.
He will dwell with them;
they will be his peoples,
and God himself will be with them;
he will wipe every tear from their eyes.
Death will be no more;
mourning and crying and pain will be no more,
for the first things have passed away.'
And the one who was seated on the throne said, 'See, I am making all things new.'

Revelation 21.1–5

Other Readings   Mothercare
A series of reflections around the death of someone suffering from dementia – from *Watching for the Kingfisher*, pages 100–110, by Ann Lewin.

We shall not be overcome
From *Enfolded in Love – Daily readings with Julian of Norwich*

He did not say, 'You shall not be tempest-tossed, you shall not be work-weary, you shall not be discomforted.' But he said,

'You shall not be overcome.' God wants us to heed these words so that we shall always be strong in trust, both in sorrow and in joy.

Sermon/Address

Song

1 Though our tears may last the night
Sorrow putting sleep to flight
While our dreams are far and few
God is making all things new
Joy will come with morning dew
God is making all things new

2 Though confusion leads to fear
Things once veiled are now made clear
What was false is now made true
God is making all things new
We recall and we review
God is making all things new

3 Shades of memories unwind
Painting pictures in our mind
Colours rich in every hue
God is making all things new
Love and hope are woven through
God is making all things new

Text © Jan Brind 2006
See original music in 'Music Supplement' on page 239 or sing to Heathlands (God of mercy, God of grace)

Prayers

Thanksgiving for the life of the departed
Lord, we are gathered here today to give thanks for the life of N and to remember *him/her*. *He/she* is now at peace and with you – *his/her* struggle is over. We give thanks for memories of N, both good and difficult.
We pray to God,
For in God all things are made new.

Prayer for those who mourn

Lord, we pray for the family and friends of N and ask you to be close to us in our grief. May the night time of our tears turn to the joy of morning as difficult memories fade and good memories take their place. We give thanks for the patience and understanding of N's carers, recognizing that they, too, are mourning *his/her* death.

We pray to God.

For in God all things are made new.

Lord, we give thanks for doctors, nurses and counsellors who work with people affected by dementia, and for the support they give to their families. We pray for continuing medical research into the cause and cure of dementia.

We pray to God.

For in God all is made new.

Prayer of penitence

Lord, we are sorry for the things we have done which we now regret. We are sorry for the times we have been impatient with N and lacked understanding. We are sorry for unhelpful words we have spoken to N and to each other in the pain of the moment. We know we could not have coped alone and yet we have feelings of guilt and failure because of our need to rely on others. We offer these feelings to God.

We pray to God,

For in God all is made new.

Prayer for readiness to live in the light of eternity

Lord, we give thanks that N is now healed and rests with you in peace, surrounded and welcomed by all your saints in heaven. We pray that we may live this life in the light of your love so that we, too, may join with the saints and be reunited with N for eternity.

We pray to God,

For in God all is made new.

The Lord's Prayer

Commendation

The Dismissal	In our tears and in our mourning **God is with us.**
	In our joy and in our re-membering **God is with us.**
	We go from this place knowing that God is with us. **Thanks be to God.**
Suggested hymns and songs	**Be still, my soul** (*Be Still and Know*) **Come to me** (*Celtic Hymn Book*) **Comfort, comfort now my people** (*Common Ground*) **Dear Lord and Father of mankind** (*Hymns Old and New – New Anglican Edition*) **God is making all things new** (*See 'Music Supplement' on page 238*) **God to enfold you** (*Iona Abbey Music Book*) **Going home** (*Be Still and Know*) **Hear me, dear Lord** (*Church Hymnary*) **In God alone my soul** (*Be Still and Know*) **In heavenly love abiding** (*Hymns Old and New: One Church, One Faith, One Lord*) **Lord of all hopefulness** (*Hymns Old and New – New Anglican Edition*) **Now the green blade riseth** (*Hymns Old and New – New Anglican Edition*) **O God, you search me** (*Christ Be Our Light*) **We cannot measure** (*When Grief is Raw*) **Within our darkest night** (*Songs from Taizé*)

Suggested Music

A Clare benediction
CD: *Gloria: The Sacred Music of John Rutter*, John Rutter, Hyperion

Pie Jesu
CD: *Requiem*, Karl Jenkins, EMI

The cloud's veil
CD: *The Cloud's Veil*, Liam Lawton, GIA Publications

Darkness is gone
CD: *God Never Sleeps: Songs from the Iona Community*, The Cathedral Singers, GIA Publications

In our tears
CD: *Dreamcatcher*, Secret Garden, Philips

Action

Make a memory board in advance of the service. (See 'How to Make a Patchwork "Memory" Banner' on page 188.) Several days before the service ask people for photos of the person who has died. These can be from all sorts of occasions and depict events from the person's life. Also, ask people to write down their special thoughts and memories about the person. Arrange the photos and pieces of script on a large display board and place it in the church where everyone can see it.

Ask people coming to the service to bring a photo or written memory with them – these can be placed on a board as they arrive.

During the service ask people to turn to each other and share one difficult memory and one good memory of the person.

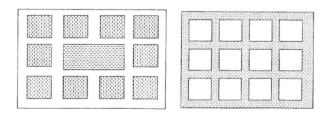

AFTER THE DEATH OF A YOUNG PERSON

Here are resources for a service to celebrate and give thanks for the life of a young person. The service is suitable for use after a sudden and unexpected death – maybe after an accident, suicide or sudden illness. At the heart and centre of this service are the siblings and young friends of the deceased. This is a service which allows young people to celebrate the life of their friend in a dignified but contemporary way. Because it is not a funeral service there can be some time before the service to plan what will happen. Some of these plans might well involve a large number of people. See the ideas below.

Preparation – some ideas

The space

Before the service starts prepare the space for the gathering. If there are chairs, arrange them in a semicircle around the focal point. Make the space feel informal. If the service is in a church remember that young people may feel very daunted about coming in to the building, so make them feel as comfortable as possible. If there is a solid wooden door into the church make sure that someone is there to open it, to greet people and to show them where to sit.

Speakers at the service

Ask some of those coming, either friends or family or those involved in the deceased's life, to speak at the service. This will have to be planned in advance and it is wise to write down what is going to be said. Choose several people and allow them, together, to discuss who will speak and about which aspects of the deceased's life. Each person should speak for no more than a few minutes.

Writing

Invite the friends and family to write poems or prayers that can be read out at the service.

Items or pictures

When the announcement about the service is made, ask everyone to bring something that reminds them of the young person who has died. This can be something they have written or drawn, or photographs or another item.

Photos

Print some large photos of the deceased and place them on or around the focal point.

Service sheet

Prepare a service sheet so everyone knows what is going to happen.

Altar or table frontal

Make an 'altar' or 'table' frontal with simple words on it like 'We remember *N* with love', 'We thank God for *N*'s life', or 'We thank God that we knew *N*'. (See 'How to Make a Paper Altar Frontal' on page 170, and 'How to Put a Design on to an Altar Frontal' on page 171.) This can be made by some of the deceased's friends, maybe using 'graffiti writing'. If the deceased had a 'tag', that can be used.

A quilt

Before the service ask everyone to make a 'quilt' square. (See 'How to Make a Patchwork "Memory" Banner' on page 188.). This can be made in either paper or fabric. Ask everyone to put something on their square that reminds them of the deceased. Make sure that everyone makes their square the same size. T-shirt inkjet transfer paper can also be used to put pictures or designs onto quilt squares. Put the 'quilt' together before the service and place it somewhere prominent in the church. The quilt can be given to the bereaved family after the service.

Balloons

On arrival at the service give everyone a helium-filled balloon tied with a ribbon. Place a card on the end of the ribbon and ask everyone to write something about the deceased on the card. The balloons can be released or everyone can give their balloon to someone else, so everyone reads someone else's card, or the balloon can be taken home.

Candles

Give everyone a candle when they arrive in the church. Have a supply of permanent marker pens and invite everyone to write a message on their candle. Invite them to write about their memory of the deceased. During the service everyone can light their candle and place it on the 'altar'.

OR

If everyone is going to put something down, invite them when they do this to pick up a candle. Suggest that they take it home and light it at a certain time, pointing out that there will then be many candles burning in different homes as people remember the deceased.

OR

Decorate chunky candles with the person's name and suitable words. These can be placed around the church and small nightlights can be put around them as part of the liturgy. (See 'How to Put a Design on to a Candle' on page 191.)

Doves

Rent some doves to be released at the end of the service, a beautiful symbol of the spirit being released from the body and flying free (see 'Useful Websites').

Favourite music

Plan to use some of the deceased's favourite music, using a CD or live music. Ask the friends or family to help choose the music.

Memorial cards

Invite everyone to write something on a memorial card. Give the cards to the deceased's family at the end of the service. (See 'Designs for Memorial Cards' on pages 205–207.)

Flowers

As people come into the building give them a flower. Have empty vases placed on the 'altar'. At a given point in the service invite everyone to put their single flower in one of the vases. Use this to illustrate that no one is alone in their grieving. As the vases fill up we see that there are many gathered together to share their grief.

PowerPoint photos

Collect together digital photos of the person's life and show these as part of the service.

The Gathering

Welcome

Introduction

Opening Responses	When understanding is gone, and confusion overwhelms, **Remember you are not alone.**
	When nothing makes sense and pain seems all around, **Remember you are not alone.**
	When life feels fragile and not so secure, **Remember you are not alone.**
	Remember we are all together, **And together we will get through.**
Bible Readings	**Jesus wept**
	When Jesus saw her weeping, and the Jews who had come along with her also weeping, he was deeply moved in spirit and troubled. 'Where have you laid him?' he asked. 'Come and see, Lord,' they replied. Jesus wept. Then the Jews said, 'See how he loved him!'
	John 11.33–36
	Love one another
	A new command I give you: love one another. As I have loved you, so you must love one another.
	John 13.34
	Live in peace with everyone
	Rejoice with those who rejoice; mourn with those who mourn. Live in harmony with one another. Do not be proud, but be willing to associate with people of low position. Do not be

conceited. Do not repay anyone evil for evil. Be careful to do what is right in the eyes of everybody. If it is possible, as far as it depends on you, live at peace with everyone. Do not take revenge, my friends, but leave room for God's wrath, for it is written: 'It is mine to avenge; I will repay', says the Lord. On the contrary: 'If your enemy is hungry, feed him; if he is thirsty, give him something to drink. In doing this, you will heap burning coals on his head.' Do not be overcome by evil, but overcome evil with good.

Romans 12.15–21

Nothing can separate us from the love of God

For I am convinced that neither death nor life, neither angels nor demons, neither the present nor the future, nor any powers, neither height nor depth, nor anything else in all creation, will be able to separate us from the love of God that is in Christ Jesus our Lord.

Romans 8.38–39

Other Readings

You'll Never Walk Alone
Oscar Hammerstein II written for the 1945 Broadway musical play Carousel.
(Available to view on the internet, see page x.)

We remember them
From *The Gates of Prayer*, a Reform Jewish prayer book published by the Central Conference.
(Available to view on the internet, see page x.)

What is dying?
Bishop Brent
(Available to view on the internet, see page x.)

He whom we love and lose is no longer where he was before; he is now wherever we are.
St John Chrysostom

Grief is not for ever, but love is.
Anon.

We can shed tears that they have gone
Anon.

We can shed tears that they have gone,
or we can smile that they have lived.
We can close our eyes and pray that they will come back,
or we can open our eyes and see all the good that they have
    left us.
Our hearts can be empty because we cannot see them,
or our hearts can be full with the love that we've shared.
We can turn our backs on tomorrow and live yesterday,
or we can be happy for tomorrow, *because* of yesterday.
We can remember them and only that they have gone,
or we can cherish their memory and let it live on.
We can cry and close our minds,
be empty and turn our backs,
or we can do what they would have wanted:
smile, open our eyes, love and go on.

The only way
Tessa Wilkinson

The only way we can be protected from the pain of loss and
the grief we feel, is by having never loved. How empty our lives
would be, and what a lot of wonderful shared moments we
would have missed, if we had not known N. So, although what
we feel at the moment is terrible, we must try to remember that
it is because we have all been privileged to have known and
loved N, that we now feel the pain and sadness.

Prayers

*Each person, or people, stand up and say the relevant line and then sit down
again*

All together   **Thank you God for N's life**
Thank you for N being *our/my son/daughter*
Thank you for N being *our/my grandchild*
Thank you for N being *my/our brother/sister*
Thank you for N being *my/our friend*
Thank you for N being *in our football team*
Thank you for N being *our colleague*

Thank you for N being . . .
Continue with suitable lines

Stand up and say together

We all knew N, and our lives were enriched by that knowing.
Thank you, God, for N's life and the way it touched our lives.
May *his/her* memory live on in all of us for ever.
Amen

When a young person dies we want to scream and shout, 'Why God? Why now? Why *him/her*? When there is so much evil in the world, when there are so many bad people, why did *he/she* have to die?'

And God looks on and knows our pain, and sadness, and anger, and sorrow. God's son Jesus also died young, and all he ever wanted was to help people love each other and be happy. And yet he died in a most terrible way. So God does understand. God reaches out and loves us, and holds us in our sadness, and walks beside us in our journey of grief. In time God helps us to make sense of what has happened and leads us to healing.

Suggested Hymns and Songs

Abide with me
(*Hymns Old and New: One Church, One Faith, One Lord*)
Brother, sister, let me serve you
(*Hymns Old and New: One Church, One Faith, One Lord*)
Going home
(*Be Still and Know*)
Guide me, O thou great redeemer
(*Hymns Ancient and Modern Revised*)
I heard the voice of Jesus say
(*Be Still and Know*)
Kindle a flame
(*Celtic Hymn Book*)
Lord, I come to you (The power of your love)
(*Hymns Old and New: One Church, One Faith, One Lord*)
Lord, the light of your love (Shine, Jesus, shine)
(*The Children's Hymn Book*)
Morning has broken
(*The Children's Hymn Book*)

We cannot measure how you heal
(*When Grief is Raw*)

Suggested Music   **Fingal's cave**
Mendelssohn

Sounds of the sea
There are many CDs produced with the natural sounds of the sea, often sold in garden centres

Bridge over troubled water
CD: *The Essential Simon and Garfunkel*, Simon and Garfunkel, Sony

Candle in the wind
CD: *Greatest Hits 1970–2002*, Elton John, Rocket

Tears in heaven
CD: *Clapton Chronicles*, Eric Clapton, Reprise Records

Fix you
CD: *Fix You*, Coldplay, Parlophone

Fields of gold
CD: *Fields of Gold*, Sting, A & M

THE SEA

Sometimes it is possible to use a seemingly unrelated subject to help reflect upon, and give insight into, another subject. The sea is one of those that can do just that. Although it has nothing to do with loss and grief, using it as an analogy to describe the journey through bereavement can work very well. This service has been designed to be used by a group of people who have come together to remember and acknowledge their shared journey of loss, which in time may lead to acceptance and inner peace.

The Gathering

Welcome

Introduction

Opening Responses	Though we feel adrift **God will not let go.**
	Though we see no light **God's light always shines.**
	Though we feel quite lost **God will show the way.**
	Though we feel despair **God's hope is still there.**
	When quite overwhelmed **God's love will bring healing and peace.**
Bible Readings	**Job cries out in his pain and distress and feels abandoned by God**
	You snatch me up and drive me before the wind; you toss me about in the storm.

I know you will bring me down to death,
to the place appointed for all the living.
Surely no-one lays a hand on a broken man
when he cries for help in his distress.
Have I not wept for those in trouble?
Has not my soul grieved for the poor?
Yet when I hoped for good, evil came;
when I looked for light, then came darkness.
The churning inside me never stops;
days of suffering confront me.
I go about blackened, but not by the sun;
I stand up in the assembly and cry for help.
I have become a brother of jackals,
a companion of owls.
My skin grows black and peels;
my body burns with fever.
My harp is tuned to mourning,
and my flute to the sound of wailing.

Job 30.22–31

People lose courage in the eye of the storm

Some went down to the sea in ships,
doing business on the mighty waters;
they saw the deeds of the LORD,
his wondrous works in the deep.
For he commanded and raised the stormy wind,
which lifted up the waves of the sea.
They mounted up to heaven, they went down to the depths;
their courage melted away in their calamity;
they reeled and staggered like drunkards,
and were at their wits' end.
Then they cried to the LORD in their trouble,
and he brought them out from their distress;
he made the storm be still,
and the waves of the sea were hushed.
Then they were glad because they had quiet,
and he brought them to their desired haven.
Let them thank the LORD for his steadfast love,
for his wonderful works to humankind.

Let them extol him in the congregation of the people,
and praise him in the assembly of the elders.

Psalm 107.23–32

Jesus calms the storm

That day when evening came, he said to his disciples, 'Let us
go over to the other side.' Leaving the crowd behind, they took
him along, just as he was, in the boat. There were also other
boats with him. A furious squall came up, and the waves broke
over the boat, so that it was nearly swamped. Jesus was in
the stern, sleeping on a cushion. The disciples woke him and
said to him, 'Teacher, don't you care if we drown?' He got up,
rebuked the wind and said to the waves, 'Quiet! Be still!' Then
the wind died down and it was completely calm. He said to his
disciples, 'Why are you so afraid? Do you still have no faith?'
They were terrified and asked each other, 'Who is this? Even
the wind and the waves obey him!'

Mark 4.35–41

Jesus walks on water and tells the disciples not to be afraid

When evening came, his disciples went down to the lake, where
they got into a boat and set off across the lake for Capernaum.
By now it was dark, and Jesus had not yet joined them. A
strong wind was blowing and the waters grew rough. When
they had rowed three or three and a half miles, they saw Jesus
approaching the boat, walking on the water; and they were
terrified. But he said to them, 'It is I; don't be afraid.' Then they
were willing to take him into the boat, and immediately the
boat reached the shore where they were heading.

John 6.16–21

Other Readings   **The sea and the beach**
Tessa Wilkinson

The sea seems to illustrate pain and sorrow so well
It comes in and goes out
For a while it is there, overwhelming, covering everything
Then slowly the tide turns and it withdraws

For a while we can see the beauty of the shells, the seaweed
We can rejoice in the patterns in the sand
We can feel the corrugated ripples under our feet
Alive to what is around, and beyond
But then the tide turns and again it is all washed away, all
      overwhelmed
We feel like the crashing of the waves on rocks
Raw and out of control
Full of anger and rage
Battered and bruised
Tossed about like flotsam floating wherever we are thrown
There are so many questions. *Why now? Why her?*
But no answers
Then the sea calms and gently the waves lap the rocks
We are soothed and the inner turmoil is calmed
In time we can learn to move up the beach as the tide comes in
Out of its reach
Not to be overwhelmed
The pain is still there, but in control
We can recognise the pain
Revisiting the sadness
Acknowledging how much the person is missed
We learn to turn away and look to the future
Knowing the person will always be part of us
Always loved and always remembered

The sea
Tessa Wilkinson

The sea is such a fickle thing
One minute smooth and calm
Blue and tranquil
The next rough and raging
Tossing anything in its path up in the air
Throwing it where it will.
So like grief
One minute we feel calm
'Today I am all right'
'Today I will not be battered and tossed about
not knowing where or who I am'

Then we see something
Or hear something
Or smell something
Quite out of the blue
And the wall of grief that we thought we had turned from
Picks us up and tosses us here and there
Until we land exhausted back on the shore

Adrift
Tessa Wilkinson

My anchor has lost its hold
I am adrift
My boat is going where it will
The sails are tattered and torn
The sea seems enormous and uncharted
It throws me hither and thither
Into the deepest, darkest trough of despair
Then up into the sunlight and for a while there is hope
Then back again into the darkness
Will my little craft be overwhelmed?
As the huge waves of grief engulf it, will it come up again?
And again and again?
They say 'time heals . . .'
Can my little boat be trimmed out with new sails?
Can it sail again into a calm harbour and put down its anchor?
Can the navigation system be mended, so I know where I am
    going?
In time, in time . . .
but not yet.
This storm has to be passed through, and then a time will come
to re-enter the harbour and return to still waters.

Grief
Tessa Wilkinson

Grief is like standing with your back to the sea
You never know when the big wave will come and
    knock you over

You'll Never Walk Alone
Oscar Hammerstein II written for the 1945 Broadway musical
play *Carousel*.
(Available to view on the internet, see page x.)

We remember them
From *The Gates of Prayer*, a Reform Jewish prayer book
published by the Central Conference
(Available to view on the internet, see page x.)

What is dying?
Bishop Brent
(Available to view on the internet, see page x.)

Footprints
Margaret Fishback Powers
(Available to view on the internet, see page x.)

Prayers

Almighty God, your love is like a great sea that girdles the
earth. Out of the deep we come to float awhile on its surface.
We cannot sound its depth or tells its greatness; only we
know that it never fails. The winds that blow over us are the
breathing of your Spirit; the sun that lights and warms us is
your truth. Sometimes you allow us to sail calm seas; now we
are buffeted by stormy waters; on the crest of the waves of
sorrow you raise us, but it is your love that bears us up; in the
trough of desolation you overwhelm us with your love on every
side. When we pass into the deep again the waters of your love
encompass and enfold us. The foolish call them the waters of
misery and death; but those who have heard the whisper of
your Spirit know them for the boundless ocean of eternal life
and love.

A prayer to go with John 6.16–21

When the storm blew up on Lake Galilee the boat felt very
small, insignificant and unsafe.

Father, when our boat seems very small and all around us
everything rocks wildly out of control, help us to feel your

loving arms holding us, until we come safely back to shore, and find our way forward onto the solid ground of your hope.

We are told that the disciples 'were terrified'.

Jesus, when we are terrified and everything seems overwhelming, when our emotions seem to control us, when we feel very alone and the way forward seems very dark, we pray that we will know you are with us, coming into our lives to show us the way. Come to us at moments when we feel most lost and overwhelmed. Dispel our fears and help us to entrust our lives to your safekeeping.

Jesus said to the disciples, 'Do not be afraid.'

Spirit of God, fall afresh on us and inspire us to go on, even when the going gets hard and we are afraid. Stir up in us an awareness of your presence, guard us and guide us, and help us to find inner peace and joy again.

A prayer to go with Psalm 107

'They mounted up to the heavens and went down to the depths,
In their peril their courage melted away.'

Our journey of grief so often goes from highs to lows.
We pray that our courage will not melt away when we find the going hard and that we will grow in hope when the moments feel a little easier.

'They reeled, they cried out to the Lord in their troubles
And he brought them out of their distress.'
Lord, when we are full of troubles and distress we pray we will turn to you to guide us from darkness to light.

'He stilled the storm to a whisper
The waves of the sea were hushed.'
Lord, we pray our journey of uncertainties will be stilled and we will find a place to rest, be still and find your peace.

The Lord's Prayer

Commendation

The Dismissal	Let us go out into the world **Blessed by this time together.**
	Let us know God's love with us **In the stormy times and the calm.**
	And may the blessing of God, Father, Son and Holy Spirit, be with us and all those whom we love today and always. **Amen**
Suggested Hymns and Songs	**Abide with me** (*Hymns Old and New: One Church, One Faith, One Lord*) **Eternal Father, strong to save** (*Hymns Old and New – New Anglican Edition*) **God moves in a mysterious way** (*Hymns Old and New – New Anglican Edition*) **Guide me, O thou great redeemer** (*Hymns Ancient and Modern Revised*) **Lead us, heavenly Father, lead us** (*Hymns Old and New – New Anglican Edition*) **Spirit of the living God** (*Hymns Old and New – New Anglican Edition*)
Suggested Music	**Fingal's cave** Mendelssohn
	Sounds of the sea There are many CDs produced with the natural sounds of the sea, often sold in garden centres
	Bridge over troubled water CD: *The Essential Simon and Garfunkel*, Simon and Garfunkel, Columbia/Legacy
Action	Write names on to stones and lay them down together, either to show that we are not alone or as if to symbolically lay down our burdens
	Make paper boats (see 'How to Make a Paper Boat' on page

190) and write names on to the sails – put down boats and pick up candles.

Decorate a large chunky candle with the words 'God's love is very great' (see 'How to Put a Design on to a Candle' on page 191). Surround this candle with small ones.

Take candles away to light our darkness.

Buy and give away copies of **Footprints** or **What is dying?**

Artwork

Design cards to pick up, illustrated with waves and a boat. (See templates on page 192.)

Make an altar frontal (see 'How to Make a Paper Altar Frontal' on page 170) and decorate it with wild waves and a small boat and the words, 'The boat may seem very small but God's love is very great', or show layers of waves, sand and rocks. (See templates on pages 192, 193 and 194.)

VALLEYS AND MOUNTAINS

Sometimes it is possible to use a seemingly unrelated subject to help reflect upon, and give insight into, another subject. Although valleys and mountains have nothing to do with loss and grief *per se*, the journey that the bereaved take is often one of repeated downs and ups. This service can be used either by a group of people who have come together to remember and acknowledge their shared journey of loss, or it can be used by a group of people who have come together to remember and give thanks for one person's life.

The Gathering

Welcome

Introduction

Opening Responses

The path up the mountain is steep and long, so like grief
Show us the way, Lord.

The path is often blocked and the way forward difficult to see, so like grief
Show us the way, Lord.

On the way we will meet friends, who will walk with us for a while
Thank you, Lord.

Eventually we will reach the summit, and all will be made clear
Praise God!
Amen

Bible Readings

God is our rock, our fort and our shield

He said:
'The LORD is my rock, my fortress, and my deliverer;
my God, my rock, in whom I take refuge,
my shield and the horn of my salvation,
my stronghold and my refuge,
my saviour; you save me from violence.
I call upon the LORD, who is worthy to be praised,
and I am saved from my enemies.

2 Samuel 22.2–4

You are my lamp

You are my lamp, O LORD;
the LORD turns my darkness into light.

2 Samuel 22.29

The Lord is my shepherd

The LORD is my shepherd, I shall not be in want.
He makes me lie down in green pastures,
he leads me beside quiet waters,
he restores my soul.
He guides me in paths of righteousness
for his name's sake.

Even though I walk
through the valley of the shadow of death,
I will fear no evil,
for you are with me;
your rod and your staff,
they comfort me.

You prepare a table before me
in the presence of my enemies.
You anoint my head with oil;
my cup overflows.
Surely goodness and love will follow me
all the days of my life,
and I will dwell in the house of the LORD for ever.

Psalm 23

God is our shelter from the storm

God is our refuge and strength,
an ever-present help in trouble.
Therefore we will not fear, though the earth give way
and the mountains fall into the heart of the sea,
though its waters roar and foam
and the mountains quake with their surging.
There is a river whose streams make glad the city of God,
the holy place where the Most High dwells.
God is within her, she will not fall;
God will help her at break of day.
Nations are in uproar, kingdoms fall;
he lifts his voice, the earth melts.

The LORD Almighty is with us;
the God of Jacob is our fortress.

Psalm 46.1–7

God will give strength to the weary and show them the way

The desert and the parched land will be glad;
the wilderness will rejoice and blossom.
Like the crocus, it will burst into bloom;
it will rejoice greatly and shout for joy.
The glory of Lebanon will be given to it,
the splendour of Carmel and Sharon;
they will see the glory of the Lord,
the splendour of our God.
Strengthen the feeble hands,
steady the knees that give way;
say to those with fearful hearts,
'Be strong, do not fear; your God will come,
he will come with vengeance;
with divine retribution
he will come to save you.'
Then will the eyes of the blind be opened
and the ears of the deaf unstopped.
Then will the lame leap like a deer,
and the mute tongue shout for joy.

Water will gush forth in the wilderness
and streams in the desert.
The burning sand will become a pool,
the thirsty ground bubbling springs.
In the haunts where jackals once lay,
grass and reeds and papyrus will grow.
And a highway will be there;
it will be called the Way of Holiness.
The unclean will not journey on it;
it will be for those who walk in that Way;
wicked fools will not go about on it.
No lion will be there,
nor will any ferocious beast get up on it;
they will not be found there.
But only the redeemed will walk there,
and the ransomed of the Lord will return.
They will enter Zion with singing;
everlasting joy will crown their heads.
Gladness and joy will overtake them,
and sorrow and sighing will flee away.

Isaiah 35

Other Readings   ### The mountains of grief
Tessa Wilkinson

How can I possibly find a way over the mountains?
I have no map, I am weak and exhausted
The path is steep and stony, and very dark
I am afraid
I don't want to go on

Preparation for a journey
Tessa Wilkinson

When we know we are going on a journey
we pack our bag and get prepared:
A guide book to tell us where to visit
A map to show us the way
A torch to light the path

Food to sustain us
Water to refresh us
Clothes to keep us warm.
But for this journey there is no time to prepare:
Just get up and go, no time to think
No guide book to tell us where we should visit
No map to show the way through grief
The light seems to fade very fast
Food seems unpalatable
Water brings no refreshment.
Wrapped in sadness we feel we walk alone

We can
Tessa Wilkinson

We can climb the highest mountains
We can visit the darkest valleys
Along the way we may feel lost, hopeless and afraid
But with friends walking beside us
We will find the way through grief
And arrive at last feeling joy in our hearts again

Firsts
Tessa Wilkinson

The journey of grief is one of 'firsts'
The first Birthday
The first Christmas
The first anniversary
The list is of endless firsts...
Each 'first' can loom ahead, huge, like a mountain to climb
A block on the way
But remember, once that 'first' is over it will never be a 'first'
    again
Next time we meet it, we will have met it before
We will know that that mountain can be climbed and we will
start to believe that we will be able to climb the next,
and the next, and the next . . .

The Five Stages of Grief
Linda Pastan
(Available to view on the internet, see page x.)

You'll Never Walk Alone
Oscar Hammerstein II written for the 1945 Broadway musical
Carousel.
(Available to view on the internet, see page x.)

We Remember Them
From *The Gates of Prayer*, a Reform Jewish prayer book
published by the Central Conference
(Available to view on the internet, see page x.)

Jesus mourns (26 May) and **God's timeless time (6 December)**
From *Bread for the Journey*, see pages 166 and 378, by Henri
J. M. Nouwen

If God sends us on stony paths he provides strong shoes.
Corrie Ten Boom
(Available to view on the internet, see page x.)

Prayers

The path is steep and rough and we have no map to show the
way.
May your guiding arms be around us, Lord.

It feels very dark, and the clouds block the view and the path
ahead.
May your light shine upon us and show us the way, Lord.

We feel very weak and unsure that we can go on.
May we feel your encouragement and love, Lord.

We feel full of fear as we walk this path alone.
**May we know as we journey on that we are never alone, and
that God will never fail us or abandon us.**

May we walk on in God's hope.
**May we arrive at the summit and know that all shall be well.
Amen**

Prayers to go with 2 Samuel 22.2–4

The Lord is my rock and my fortress. He is the One who saves me.
Thank you, Lord, for being our fortress, for surrounding us with your love when we feel vulnerable and alone.

My God is my rock. I go to him for safety.
Thank you, Lord, for being there as our rock, giving us the underpinning we need to stand firm when all around us everything feels very unsafe and new.

He is like a shield to me. He's the power that saves me.
Thank you, Lord, for the protection you give us, always there to shield and protect us from the thoughts and feelings we have which sometimes make us feel as if we will go mad with too much pain and grief.

He's my place of safety. I go to him for help. He's my Saviour. He saves me from those who want to hurt me.
Thank you, Lord, for the way you lead us to a safe place when we are struggling to cope with so many pieces of advice about how we should feel and behave. You shield us from being overwhelmed by words meant to comfort, but which often hurt.

I call out to the Lord. He is worthy of praise.
Amen

Though we see no light
God's light always shines.

Though we feel quite lost
God will show the way.

Though we feel despair
God's hope is still there.

Though we feel overwhelmed
God's love will bring healing and peace.

Use the song **Brother, sister, let me serve you** *as a prayer. The two sides of the church can say the verses alternately. Or the person leading the prayers can say the verses and the people can respond between each verse:*

Let us help each other on our journey,
Walk the road and share the pain.
OR
I will share your joys and sorrows
Till we've seen this journey through.

The Lord's Prayer

Commendation

The Dismissal   May we all go from here having been blessed by spending this
time together.
May we have gained strength to face whatever lies ahead,
strength to climb the highest mountain.
Amen

Suggested Hymns   Abide with me
and Songs   (*Hymns Old and New: One Church, One Faith, One Lord*)
Dear Lord and Father of mankind
(*Hymns Old and New – New Anglican Edition*)
Father, hear the prayer we offer
(*Hymns Old and New – New Anglican Edition*)
Guide me, O thou great redeemer
(*Hymns Ancient and Modern Revised*)
Lead us, heavenly Father, lead us
(*Hymns Old and New: New Anglican Edition*)
Lo, I am with you
(*There is One Among Us*)
Lord, I come to you (The power of your love)
(*Hymns Old and New: One Church, One Faith, One Lord*)
Lord, we pray, be near us
(*See 'Music Supplement' on page 240*)
One more step along the world I go
(*The Children's Hymn Book*)
Spirit of the living God
(*Hymns Old and New – New Anglican Edition*)

Suggested Music   **Climb every mountain**
CD: *The Sound of Music*, Rodgers and Hammerstein

Mysterious mountain
CD: *Mysterious Mountain*, Alan Hovhaness, Telarc

By my side (Where are you going?)
CD: *Godspell*, Stephen Schwartz

Action   Write names onto stones and place them together to make a cairn, to show that we are not alone.

Write names onto large stones and bring them forward, laying them down as the symbolic weight of grief. In exchange pick up candles as lights to show the way.

Light candles - if everyone has a candle the light can be passed around until all are lit and comfort can be drawn from each other's light.

Artwork   Make an altar frontal (see 'How to Make a Paper Altar Frontal' on page 170) and cover the front with a large map. On the map place the words, 'Put your hands into the hand of God' (see template on page 195).

WATER BUGS AND DRAGONFLIES

This service is based on the short book *Water Bugs and Dragonflies: Explaining Death to Children* by Doris Stickney. The service takes that theme and develops it into a complete service of remembrance. At the front of the gathering there is a table or altar. On the altar is a blue cloth and, placed on the cloth, paper water lilies and water lily leaves. On the centre of each water lily place a lit nightlight. On arrival everyone is given a pencil and a brightly coloured paper dragonfly wrapped up in a piece of brown paper. (See the templates for paper dragonflies and water lilies and water lily leaves on pages 196–199.)

The Gathering

Welcome

Introduction   We have gathered here tonight to remember and give thanks for those we have known and loved and who have now died. Our theme this evening will be based on a small book called *Water Bugs and Dragonflies*. It was written in 1982 by Doris Stickney and is a beautiful, gentle exploration of death and resurrection.

Everything you will need for the service is on the sheet. The congregation says everything **in bold print.**

Opening responses   Life has many mysteries.
We do not have all the answers.

Jesus told us he was going ahead to prepare a place for us.
Let us live as people of hope and expectation.

Hymn   Lord we pray be near us

1   Lord, we pray, be near us,
    In this time of grief;
    Bring us peace and healing,
    Solace and relief:
    Heaviness surrounds us
    Like a storm-filled cloud;
    Sounds of day and sunlight
    Now seem harsh and loud.

2   As the shadows deepen
    Chasing out the light;
    Hold us in your hand, and
    Lead us through the night:
    May we, in our sorrow,
    Feel your loving care;
    When life overwhelms us
    Know that you are near.

3   In the end we trust that
    All shall be made well;
    Send your Holy Spirit
    In our hearts to dwell:
    Gently, oh so gently,
    Day must dawn again;
    Shafts of golden sunlight
    Shining through the rain.

Text © Jan Brind 2004
See original music on page 241 or sing to Cranham (In the bleak mid-winter)

Water Bugs and Dragonflies
The story is now read out loud

Bible Readings   *Read one of these:*

There are many rooms in my Father's house

'Do not let your hearts be troubled. Believe in God, believe also in me. In my Father's house there are many dwelling-places. If it were not so, would I have told you that I go to prepare a place for you? And if I go and prepare a place for you, I will come again and will take you to myself, so that where I am, there you may be also.'

John 14.1–3

The body is buried mortal and raised immortal

So it is with the resurrection of the dead. What is sown is perishable, what is raised is imperishable. It is sown in dishonour, it is raised in glory. It is sown in weakness, it is raised in power.

1 Corinthians 15.42–43

We shall be changed and shall reign for ever and ever

Listen, I will tell you a mystery! We will not all die, but we will all be changed, in a moment, in the twinkling of an eye, at the last trumpet. For the trumpet will sound, and the dead will be raised imperishable, and we will be changed. For this perishable body must put on imperishability, and this mortal body must put on immortality. When this perishable body puts on imperishability, and this mortal body puts on immortality, then the saying that is written will be fulfilled: 'Death has been swallowed up in victory.'

1 Corinthians 15.51–54

Other Readings   **I said to the man who stood at the gate of the year**
Minnie Louise Haskins
(Available to view on the internet, see page x.)

God give them rest
Anon.

God give them rest in that delightful garden where pain and grief are no more and sighing unknown.

I believe in the sun
Words found written on a cellar wall in Cologne after World
War II

I believe in the sun even when it is not shining
I believe in love even when I feel it not
I believe in God even when he is silent.

From water bug to dragonfly
Tessa Wilkinson

The bottom of the pond is muddy and dark
There is fear of the unknown
There is loneliness as things change
There is the desperation of being left behind
Not knowing, not understanding
Watching and waiting
Then the journey comes
Up the stem
What waits beyond?
Sunlight
Freedom
Dancing together in joy with those who went before
And who will come after.

Grief is not for ever, but Love is.
Anon.

From **Rabindranath Tagore**
Death is not the extinguishing of the light, but the putting out
of the lamp because dawn has come.

On heaven
Robert E. Selle
(Available to view on the internet, see page x.)

Hymn   **Abide with me**

We have heard the story read to us of the way in which the water
bug becomes the dragonfly and then flies free into the sky. Now

we are going to re-enact this symbolically. First, by taking the dragonfly from the paper wrapping we are being reminded of our transformation from this earthly life to a new heavenly life. Then, we may name the dragonfly as the one we have loved and are remembering; we do this by writing their name on the dragonfly's wings. Finally, we may take the dragonfly and place it amongst the water lilies to remind ourselves that our loved ones have broken through the surface of the water to fly free with God.

After this the names of those being remembered tonight are read out in alphabetical order.

Stillness

Prayers

All through the New Testament, Jesus used parables to teach those around him. He told stories about everyday life events to illustrate his Good News message. The same is being done in the story of *Water Bugs and Dragonflies*; it carries a message of delight, for life after death, freedom, light and hope.

Let us pray that we will understand that message, take it into our hearts and rejoice in the wonderful freedom and new life that awaits us after we die. Free from illness, disability and pain. Washed in the light of love.

God, we feel the pain of loss and separation.
Help to heal that pain.

God, we want to believe.
Help our unbelief.

God, we want so much for our loved ones to return and tell us that all is well.
Help us to believe the message of hope that Jesus gave us.

God, we thank you for all we were given by those who have died.
Let us journey on with those memories and use them well in our lives.

God, we pray we will live our lives as if each day were a precious gift.
May we know that at our end we shall be reunited with those we have loved and who have loved us.

God, we pray that your message of new life and new hope will be one we can believe in and celebrate.
In your love, Lord, we shall have new life, new birth, and new freedom.

We offer these prayers to God our Father, in the name of Jesus, and in the power of the Holy Spirit.
Amen

The Lord's Prayer

Commendation

The Dismissal   Dear God, may we look backwards with gratitude, forwards with courage and upwards with confidence.
Amen

Go out with your life renewed in the hope of all the good things to come.
Amen

Live well and believe that all shall be well.
Amen
The blessing of God . . .

Other Hymns and Songs

Care for one another
(*Children's Praise*)
Father be with her family
(*Children's Praise*)
Father for our friends we pray
(*Children's Praise*)
Give us the wings of faith
(*Hymns Old and New – New Anglican Edition*)
Going home
(*Be Still and Know*)
Lord, the light of your love (Shine, Jesus, shine)
(*The Children's Hymn Book*)

Suggested Music   **The flight of the bumble bee**
Rimsky-Korsakov

Tears in heaven
CD: *Clapton Chronicles*, Eric Clapton, Reprise Records

Artwork and
action

Make paper dragonflies in bright
coloured paper. Wrap each one in brown paper. (See template
on page 196.)

Make paper water lilies and paper water lily leaves to put on
the altar or table. (See 'How to Make a Paper Waterlily 1' on
page 197, 'How to Make a Paper Waterlily 2' on page 198, and
leaves template on page 199.)

Make a stole decorated with dragonflies. (See 'How to Make a
Stole' on page 178, and template on page 196.)

Unwrap a paper dragonfly. Write the name/names of those being
remembered on the wings. Place on the paper water lilies.

WINTER AND SPRING

Sometimes it is possible to use a seemingly unrelated subject to help reflect upon, and give insight into, another subject. Looking at the seasons of winter and spring, which illustrate death and resurrection so well, we can do just that. Using winter and spring as an analogy to describe the journey through bereavement can work very well. This service has been designed to be used either by a group of people who have come together to remember and acknowledge their shared journey of loss, or it could be used by a group of people who have come together to remember and give thanks for one person's life. Acknowledging the new birth of spring that comes after the death of winter can help to bring understanding and peace.

The Gathering

Welcome

Introduction

Opening Responses	When winter comes and all seems dark and hope is gone, **Guide us from darkness to light.**
	When spring starts to appear, and hope is rekindled, **Bring us your comfort and show us the way.**
	When the sun shines warm, birds sing and the bulbs bloom, **Let us rejoice at the ending of winter and the signs of new hope.**
Bible Readings	**God is faithful**
	As long as the earth endures, seedtime and harvest, cold and heat, summer and winter,

day and night,
shall not cease.

Genesis 8.22

For everything there is a season

There is a time for everything,
and a season for every activity under heaven:
a time to be born and a time to die,
a time to plant and a time to uproot,
a time to kill and a time to heal,
a time to tear down and a time to build,
a time to weep and a time to laugh,
a time to mourn and a time to dance,
a time to scatter stones and a time to gather them,
a time to embrace and a time to refrain,
a time to search and a time to give up,
a time to keep and a time to throw away,
a time to tear and a time to mend,
a time to be silent and a time to speak,
a time to love and a time to hate,
a time for war and a time for peace.

Eccleciastes 3.1–8

My beloved speaks and says to me:
'Arise, my love, my fair one,
and come away;
for now the winter is past,
the rain is over and gone.
The flowers appear on the earth;
The time of singing has come,
and the voice of the turtle-dove
is heard in our land.
The fig tree puts forth its figs,
and the vines are in blossom;
They give forth fragrance.
Arise, my love, my fair one,
and come away.

The Song of Solomon 2.10–13

Benedicite – The Song of Creation

Bless the Lord sun and moon:
Bless the Lord you stars of heaven;
Bless the Lord all rain and dew:
Sing his praise and exalt him for ever.
Bless the Lord all winds that blow:
Bless the Lord you fire and heat;
Bless the Lord scorching wind and bitter cold:
Sing his praise and exalt him for ever.
Bless the Lord dews and falling snows:
Bless the Lord you nights and days;
Bless the Lord light and darkness:
Sing his praise and exalt him for ever.
Bless the Lord frost and cold:
Bless the Lord you ice and snow;
Bless the Lord lightnings and clouds:
Sing his praise and exalt him for ever.

taken from The Song of the Three, vv 4–7

Other Readings

Winter and spring
Tessa Wilkinson

When winter comes, spring will not be far behind.

Ice
Tessa Wilkinson

The ice on the pond looks solid and sound
A tentative step onto the edge proves safe
Further out cracking noises beneath my feet
Deep threatening darkness below the ice
Fear, fast beating heart, run
Run back, back to the bank
To safety
To the place I know of solid rock.
So like visiting grief
Tiptoe to the edge of sadness and sorrow
Test the emotions, will they hold?
Will cracks appear, and the threat of breaking be too much to
    bear?

Will the place they might lead to be too dark and dangerous?
Will I trust I can make it back to my solid rock again?
Can I trust that all shall be well?

Snow
Tessa Wilkinson

The snow arrived unannounced
It overwhelmed everything
Changed the landscape so it was unrecognisable
No one was prepared
My grief feels like that snowstorm
I feel changed, weighed down by the burden
Trying to negotiate the new environment around me
Not knowing where I am going
Looking for familiar landmarks
I feel cold and miserable and ill equipped in this new place
unvisited before
But I know in time the snow will melt and return the landscape
to some semblance of normality
And I know in time my grief will diminish and I will find my
way forward again, back to a world that I recognise, changed,
but familiar
Spring does always come after winter and hope will return

Sharing
Brenda Lismer
From *All in the End is Harvest*, page 20, edited by Agnes
Whitaker.

The Leaves
Adapted from *Bambi* by Felix Saltern. This can be read by two
voices.

The leaves were falling from the trees. Two leaves clung on. 'It
isn't the way it used to be,' said one leaf to the other.
'No, so many of us have fallen off tonight, we're almost the
only two left on this branch,' answered the other.
'Even when it is warm and the sun shines, a storm or a cloud
burst would come sometimes, and many leaves would be torn
off, though they were still young. You never know who is going
to go next.'

'The sun seldom shines now,' sighed the second leaf. 'Soon we will go. Can it be true that we are replaced by others, and then, when they have gone, by others, more and more?'

'It is really true,' whispered the other leaf. 'It makes me feel very sad. Why must we all fall? What happens to us once we have fallen?'

'We sink down . . . what do you think is under us?'

'I don't know, some say one thing, and some another, but nobody knows. No one has ever come back to tell us about it.'

'Which of us will go first?'

'Let's not worry about that now, let's remember how beautiful it was, how wonderful when the sun came out and shone so warmly that we thought we'd burst with life. Do you remember?'

'Yes I remember, but look at me now, I am so yellow and ugly.'

'No, you are as lovely as the day that you were born.'

Hours passed, a moist wind blew cold and hostile through the branches.

The leaves were torn from their places and spun downwards . . . winter had come.

Look to this day
From the Sanskrit

Look well to this day! For it is life,
The very life of life.
For yesterday is but a dream
And tomorrow is only a vision:
But today well lived
Makes every yesterday a dream of happiness
And every tomorrow a vision of hope –
Look well therefore to this day
Such is the salutation of the dawn.

Prayers

God of Comfort,
we hold out to you all here today who feel that winter has come now that their loved one has died. We pray that in time they will know that spring always follows winter. That the cold

dark place of grief will gradually melt and be warmed by your healing, warming love and peace.
Lord, share our sadness
And bring us healing and peace.

God of Friendship,
we hold out to you all here today who feel alone and afraid, uncertain what their future will hold. We pray that they will be aware of you walking beside them, guiding and guarding them and leading them on to a new place, and a new hope.
Lord, hold our loneliness
And bring us healing and peace.

God of Love,
we hold out to you all those gathered here today who feel frightened by change and newness. As the world around us is ever changing, moving from season to season, we pray that we may grow to trust that in our lives, although many things change, God's love will never change and will always be there for us.
Lord, enfold us in your love
And bring us healing and peace.

The Lord's Prayer

Commendation

The Dismissal   May the God of winter meet us in our dark nights and show us the way.
May the God of spring bless us with a message of hope and healing.
May we all be blessed by the knowledge that spring always follows winter.
And may we all live in the light and warming love of the risen Lord.
Amen

Suggested Hymns   **In the bulb there is a flower**
and Songs   (*Church Hymnary*)
                      Now the green blade riseth
                      (*Hymns Old and New – New Anglican Edition*)

Lord of all hopefulness
(*Hymns Old and New – New Anglican Edition*)
Do not be afraid
(*Be Still and Know*)
We cannot care for you the way we wanted
(*When Grief is Raw*)
When Jesus longed for us to know
(*Church Hymnary*)

Suggested Music   **Turn! Turn! Turn (To everything there is a season)**
The Byrds

Four seasons
Vivaldi

Circle of life
CD: *Gift of God*, Marty Haugen, GIA Publications

Circle me Lord
CD: *Sacred Weave*, Keith Duke, Kevin Mayhew

To everything there is a season
CD: *Gloria: The Sacred Music of John Rutter*, John Rutter, Hyperion

Action   Scatter a handful of dried leaves beneath the altar and pick up a spring bulb or some sunflower seeds.

Write the names of those being remembered on dried leaves, scatter the leaves beneath the altar and pick up a spring bulb or a candle.

Artwork   Make an altar frontal (see 'How to Make a Paper Altar Frontal' on page 170, and templates on pages 201 and 202) and decorate with leaves and spring bulbs.

PART 4: BURIAL OF ASHES AND TIMES TO REMEMBER

BURIAL OF ASHES

If a person has been cremated, then at some time the next of kin will have to decide what they want to do with the ashes. Usually the ashes will be held by the crematorium or the undertaker until that decision is made. Often the family will be contacted to ask what they want to happen to them. Today the options are many and varied, but most people will ask for the ashes to be buried or scattered. Where and how this happens then has to be decided. For some people there is a sense of wanting to get it 'over and done with' as soon as possible, but for others keeping the ashes either at home or with the undertaker is the chosen option, because they feel they are in no hurry to say the final 'Goodbye'. As with so many decisions that have to be made around the time of death and afterwards, there is no one right answer about the timing, or about what to do. So what are the options?

- Burial in the local churchyard or cemetery.
- Burial at crematorium.
- Burial in a 'green site' or Woodland Trust property.
- Burial somewhere significant.
- Scattering of ashes in churchyard or cemetery.
- Scattering of ashes somewhere significant.
- Scattering of ashes at sea.
- Scattering of ashes from a plane.
- Scattering of ashes using fireworks.
- Making ashes into a carbon 'diamond'.
- Doing nothing and keeping the ashes at home.

Whichever decision is made, permission may have to be sought from the appropriate authority. Some churches insist that ashes are buried in a container, urn or casket, while others allow them to tipped out of the container and put directly into a hole. Most churches or authorities will say that the ashes must be covered by soil: they are not allowed to be scattered or strewn. So it is important to find out what the rules and regulations are in each area. The reason for burying ashes will vary from person to person. It may be so they can visit the burial site in the future, or they may want to put up a memorial on the site, or it may enable them to put the ashes of more than one family member together.

The service

The 'service' for the disposal or burial of ashes is very short and few words are needed or given. Because not many words are said, it is important that the ones used do have meaning for those gathered together to say their final farewell.

The service is a time to commend the person who has died to God's care and to commit their remains to the earth.

Sentences

The famous words 'Earth to earth, ashes to ashes, dust to dust' are often used. Other short sentences can be written to suit the occasion:

- 'We pray that our sorrow may be turned to joy, our pain to peace, our loss to hope.'
- 'Bulbs to plants, plants to flowers, winter to spring, death to resurrection.'
- 'Uncertainty to certainty, questions to answers, despair to hope, hope to new life.'
- 'Loneliness to friendship, friendship to love, love to joy restored.'
- 'Darkness to light, fear to trust, despair to hope, hope to new life.'

Bible Readings   **A thousand years in your sight**

Lord, you have been our dwelling-place
in all generations.
Before the mountains were brought forth,
or ever you had formed the earth and the world,
from everlasting to everlasting you are God.

You turn us back to dust,
and say, 'Turn back, you mortals.'
For a thousand years in your sight
are like yesterday when it is past,
or like a watch in the night.

You sweep them away; they are like a dream,
like grass that is renewed in the morning;
in the morning it flourishes and is renewed;
in the evening it fades and withers.
Psalm 90.1–6

Let the children come to me

People were bringing little children to Jesus to have him touch them, but the disciples rebuked them. When Jesus saw this, he was indignant. He said to them, 'Let the little children come to me, and do not hinder them, for the kingdom of God belongs to such as these. I tell you the truth, anyone who will not receive the kingdom of God like a little child will never enter it.' And he took the children in his arms, put his hands on them and blessed them.
Mark 10.13–16

In my Father's house

Do not let your hearts be troubled. Trust in God; trust also in me. In my Father's house are many rooms; if it were not so, I would have told you. I am going there to prepare a place for you. And if I go and prepare a place for you, I will come back and take you to be with me that you also may be where I am.
John 14.1–3

Love

If I speak in the tongues of mortals and of angels, but do not have love, I am a noisy gong or a clanging cymbal. And if I have prophetic powers, and understand all mysteries and all knowledge, and if I have all faith, so as to remove mountains, but do not have love, I am nothing. If I give away all my possessions, and if I hand over my body so that I may boast, but do not have love, I gain nothing.

Love is patient; love is kind; love is not envious or boastful or arrogant or rude. It does not insist on its own way; it is not irritable or resentful; it does not rejoice in wrongdoing, but rejoices in the truth. It bears all things, believes all things, hopes all things, endures all things.

Love never ends. But as for prophecies, they will come to an end; as for tongues, they will cease; as for knowledge, it will come to an end. For we know only in part, and we prophesy only in part; but when the complete comes, the partial will come to an end.

When I was a child, I spoke like a child, I thought like a child, I reasoned like a child; when I became an adult, I put an end to childish ways. For now we see in a mirror, dimly, but then we will see face to face. Now I know only in part; then I will know fully, even as I have been fully known. And now faith, hope, and love abide, these three; and the greatest of these is love.

1 Corinthians 13.1–13

The Dismissal   We pray that we will feel God with us as we leave this place to journey on without N. Our way forward is unknown and frightening. Our emptiness and sadness can feel very overwhelming, but, with God at our side guiding us forward, we can come through the fear and know inner peace again.
Amen

May we be enveloped in God's love and peace.
May we feel God's presence with us whenever we face difficult times.
May we continue to rejoice together as we remember all that N gave to us.
Let us go in the love of Christ.
Amen

Though we feel very alone
God is with us.
Though we feel overwhelmed
God is with us.
Though we wonder how we will cope
God is with us.

God is in our past
and in our future,
in our fears
and in our hopes,

in our tears
and in our laughter.
God is above us and below us
God surrounds us
and enfolds us with love,
light and peace.
Amen

Suggested Hymns and Songs

Although outside, it may be possible to ask someone to either sing a solo piece, or to lead the people in singing an unaccompanied hymn or song

God to enfold you
(*Iona Abbey Music Book*)
Lord Jesus Christ
(*Songs from Taizé*)
May the Lord bless you (Margaret Rizza)
(*Be Still and Know*)
The Lord bless you and keep you (John Rutter)
(*Sheet music from Oxford University Press*)
The Lord's my shepherd
(*Hymns Old and New: One Church, One Faith, One Lord*)
The peace of the earth
(*There is One Among Us*)

Action   Here are suggestions for actions suitable for use during a burial of ashes. One of these may add a little more to the occasion.

Drawstring bag
Before the service make a cotton drawstring bag (see 'How to Make a Drawstring Bag to Hold Ashes' on page 203). Listed below are somes ideas for designs to go on the bag. Place the ashes in the bag before the ceremony. Place the bag by the hole before everyone arrives. When it comes to the time to bury the ashes, place the bag in the hole. The fabric used for the bag should be a natural fabric like cotton so it is biodegradable. The design of the fabric could reflect the person who has died.

- Small flowers or nursery fabric for a child.
- A computer transfer photo of the person.
- The person's initials.
- Fabric with a design on it that reflects something about the person's life.
- A bag made from a much-loved piece of clothing – maybe a wedding dress, or a special outfit recently worn.

Invite the people there to fill in the hole
Take a collection of trowels with you so that anyone there, who wants to, can help fill in the hole, or have earth in a basket for people to place in the hole.

Bury bulbs or seeds
As the hole that the ashes have been put into is filled in, invite those gathered there to bury some bulbs or seeds in the soil. The plants will grow and flower later in the year and in following years – a wonderful way to illustrate death and resurrection.

Dried autumn leaves
In the autumn collect some beautiful autumn leaves and dry them under something heavy so they are flat. After the hole has been dug place them carefully in a pattern around and in the hole.

Pebbles or shells
Collect pebbles or shells and place them around the hole in a beautiful pattern. If there are children in the family who are involved in the burial, they might like to help with the arrangement.

A REFLECTIVE QUIET TIME AFTER A MISCARRIAGE

After a miscarriage the sadness of the loss of a baby can be very acute; but because, for the outside world, it may seem like an insignificant event, the sadness and loss are often not acknowledged. This short time of reflection gives the family a chance to say goodbye and to mark the death of their baby. It might happen around a hospital bed or just at the family home. A lit decorated candle might be placed on a table to bring the Light of Christ into the centre of the room. (See 'How to Put a Design on to a Candle' on page 191.)

Some parents have a strong sense of the gender of their baby, and will have chosen a name; or they might choose a name that could be either gender, like Jo or Sam. Some will have had a nickname for the child. If they do have a name, it is important to use it during this shared time together. This will help the family to feel that the baby is part of their family for ever.

Welcome	We come here today to reflect for a moment on the life that is gone, to say goodbye to your baby, and to ask that you will feel God's healing love and peace with you at all times as you journey on.
Opening Responses	Lord, we feel so lost and overwhelmed. **Hear us in our pain and confusion.** Lord, our baby has died. **Hear us in our pain and confusion.** Lord, we had such hopes and expectations. **Hear us in our pain and confusion.**

Our child who has died was precious to us and precious to God.
Lord, hear us in our pain and confusion.

Bible Readings

Jesus shows his love for children

People were bringing little children to him in order that he might touch them; and the disciples spoke sternly to them. But when Jesus saw this, he was indignant and said to them, 'Let the little children come to me; do not stop them; for it is to such as these that the kingdom of God belongs. Truly I tell you, whoever does not receive the kingdom of God as a little child will never enter it.' And he took them up in his arms, laid his hands on them, and blessed them.

Mark 10.13–16

Nothing can separate us from the love of God

For I am convinced that neither death, nor life, nor angels, nor rulers, nor things present, nor things to come, nor powers, nor height, nor depth, nor anything else in all creation, will be able to separate us from the love of God in Christ Jesus our Lord.

Romans 8. 38–39

Other readings

Grief
Anon.

Grief is not for ever, but love is.

Love
Tessa Wilkinson

You were conceived in love
Grew surrounded by our love
Died enfolded by love
Love never dies

We trust
Anon.

We trust that beyond absence there is a presence.

That beyond the pain there can be healing.
That beyond the brokenness there can be wholeness.
That beyond the anger there may be peace.
That beyond the hurting there may be forgiveness.
That beyond the silence there may be the word.
That beyond the word there may be understanding.
That through understanding there is love.

Lost love
Copyright © Anne M. R. Chiles, 2000, used with permission
from the Miscarriage Association

A kiss never kissed
A dream never wished
An embrace never felt
A beauty never beheld
A tear never cried
A life never tried
A love never shown
A child never known

Prayers

Father God, Mother God, at this time of deep sadness and pain, we hold N and N out to you as they try to make sense of what has happened. They had been so excited and now their baby/N has died. All their hopes are shattered, all their joys replaced by despair. We pray that you will hold them in your loving arms. We pray that their family and friends will comfort them, and, as the days pass, we pray that the pain of loss may diminish and be replaced by healing and joy.

When a miscarriage has robbed us of a child,
when all seems out of control,
when life seems so vulnerable,
when our beliefs are shaken:
Be near us, Lord.

When we feel our bodies have let us down,
when we feel we have failed,
when we want to stop but have to carry on,
when people around don't understand:
Be near us, Lord.

When we take the risk to try again,
when everything inside says 'Don't' and we do,
when the blue line shows up on the pregnancy test:
Be near us, Lord.

Father God, Mother God, you know what it is like to have a child die.
Come alongside N and N and all those who have had a baby die.
Give them the strength to carry on,
the hope that all shall be well,
the knowledge of your love,
and your blessing today and always.
Amen

Artwork or actions

Decorate a candle with the name of the child and suitable words such as 'N, *we will always love you*', 'N, *rest in peace*' or 'N, *you will always be part of our family*' (see 'How to Put a Design on to a Candle' on page 191). This candle can be lit during the brief 'service' and kept by the family to light at appropriate times. Make it clear to the family that if they burn the candle, another can easily be made to replace it.

As part of the time together plant a rose bush or small tree in the garden in memory of the child.

Buy a plain glass vase and decorate it with similar words to the candle. The family can fill it with flowers in memory of their child. Glass paint can be bought in craft shops.

Remember to be in touch with the family around the time that the child would have been born, either by visiting or sending a card.

'TIME TO REMEMBER' IN PARISHES

Many parish churches hold regular 'Time to Remember' services, either once a year around the time of All Souls, or more frequently throughout the year. We hope that the resources in the Memorial and Thanksgiving services in this book will help those planning such services. Below is a general list of readings, hymns, songs, music and actions that might be appropriate for such services.

Bible Readings 2 Samuel 22.2–4: The Lord is my rock
Psalm 23: The Lord is my shepherd
Psalm 42: My soul longs for you, O God
Psalm 139: O God, you search me
Ecclesiastes 3.1–8: For everything there is a season
Isaiah 43.1–7: Do not be afraid
Wisdom of Solomon 3.1–9: The souls of the righteous
Matthew 5.1–11: The Beatitudes
Matthew 11.25–30: Come to me
John 14.1–3: There are many rooms in my Father's house
John 15.9–17: Love one another
Romans 8.38–39: Nothing can separate us from the love of God
1 Corinthians 13.1–13: Love
Revelation 21.1–5a: He will wipe away every tear from their eyes

Other Readings From *The Prophet*, Kahlil Gibran

Your pain is the breaking of the shell that encloses your understanding. Even as the stone of the fruit must break, that its heart may stand in the sun, so must you know pain.

The following readings are all available to view on the internet (see page x).

Footprints
Margaret Fishback Powers

Love Lingers
Richard Fife

We remember them
From *The Gates of Prayer*, a Reform Jewish Prayer book published by the Central Office

I said to the man who stood at the gate of the year
Minnie Louise Haskins

You'll never walk alone
Oscar Hammerstein II written for the 1945 Broadway musical play *Carousel*

Hymns and Songs **Be still, my soul**
(*Be Still and Know*)
Brother, sister, let me serve you
(*Hymns Old and New: One Church, One Faith, One Lord*)
Christ's is the world (A touching place)
(*When Grief is Raw*)
Dear Lord and Father of mankind
(*Hymns Old and New – New Anglican Edition*)
Everyday God
(*Restless is the Heart*)
Father, hear the prayer we offer
(*Hymns Old and New – New Anglican Edition*)
God to enfold you
(*Iona Abbey Music Book*)
Holy God, to you we cry
(*See 'Music Supplement' on page 242*)
I heard the voice of Jesus say
(*Be Still and Know*)
Let there be love shared among us
(*Hymns Old and New – New Anglican Edition*)

Lord, we pray be near us
(*See 'Music Supplement' on page 240*)
My peace I leave you
(*Cantate*)
Nothing can trouble (Nada te turbe)
(*Songs From Taizé*)
O God, you search me
(*Christ, Be Our Light*)
O what their joy and their glory must be
(*Complete Anglican Hymns Old and New*)
Thanks be to God
(*Hymns Old and New: One Church, One Faith, One Lord*)
There's a wideness in God's mercy
(*Complete Anglican Hymns Old and New*)
Watch, O Lord
(*Turn My Heart*)
We cannot measure
(*When Grief is Raw*)

Music

As well as classical music and the individual tracks listed in the different services of this book, look at the 'Useful CDs' section at the back of the book. There are many pieces of music that are suitable to play before, during, or after a 'Time to Remember' service.

Actions

With candles
Candles and drip-shields can be given to everyone to light during the service as a symbol that we are together in our grief, and the light of Christ is around us.
Nightlights can be in a basket by the altar to be lit by people during the service.
Nightlights can be given to be taken away and lit at home.

With butterflies
Brightly coloured butterfly shapes can be wrapped in pieces of brown paper. During the service, people are invited to 'release' their butterflies and write names being remembered on the white spaces. The butterflies are then brought forward and placed on the altar, or in a basket, hung from a tree, or taken home (see page 176 for template).

With flowers

Everyone can be given a flower when they arrive – these are put in an empty vase on the altar during the service to show that we are not alone.

With photographs

Ask people to bring a photograph of the person who has died and place these on the altar – make cardboard easels to display the photos. (See 'How to Make an Easel' on page 204.)

With balloons

Use helium-filled balloons – either release them, or write messages on them and take them home. They might be given to someone who was not at the service.

With doves

Rent some doves to be released at the service – spirits flying free (see 'Useful Websites').

With memory cards

Design cards for people to write names on. Either place these on the altar by a lit candle or take home. Possible card designs include doves, flowers, butterflies, dragonflies, leaves, candles. (See 'How to Make an Easel for a Card Display' on page 204, and templates on pages 205, 206 and 207.)

With stones

Write names on stones and ask people to build a cairn together. As well as being a corporate action of togetherness, this shows so well that we are not alone. Placing a stone on a cairn is also a way of laying down a burden.

With leaves

Write names on leaves to lay at the altar and pick up a bulb to take home and plant – symbolic of death and resurrection – or collect a candle to take home.

Scatter leaves and pick up sunflower seeds to grow at home.

'TIME TO REMEMBER' IN HOSPITALS AND HOSPICES

Hospitals and hospices regularly hold memorial or 'Time to Remember' services for specific groups – stillbirth, children, road traffic accidents, cot deaths – as well as regular memorial services for the bereaved.

These services often have to meet the needs of people of faith, or none. This needs careful thought, especially as the services are usually planned by the Christian chaplaincy. Many hospitals and hospices do now have interfaith pastoral support teams who will know the needs of their particular communities.

One way to embrace the groups of those with faith and those with none is to hold an event that has three parts. The first part can be secular. It is during this that the names of those being remembered are read out. There can be secular readings and music and a symbolic action. The next part consists of a time of refreshment and an opportunity to meet each other. The final part can be a faith-based liturgy. Planning the event in this way means that people who do not want to stay for the final act of worship can leave after the refreshment.

Resources from the memorial and thanksgiving services, as well as the suggestions in 'Time to Remember in Parishes', can be adapted and used for these 'remembering' events.

PART FIVE: RESOURCES FOR CREATING SERVICES

HOW TO MAKE

FRONT SERVICE SHEET WITH BUTTERFLY DESIGN 1

FRONT SERVICE SHEET WITH BUTTERFLY DESIGN 2

FRONT SERVICE SHEET WITH BUTTERFLY DESIGN 3

THE FUNERAL SERVICE OF

XXXXXX

XX/XX/XX

ALWAYS REMEMBERED
WITH FONDEST LOVE

HOW TO MAKE A PAPER ALTAR FRONTAL

1 Take a roll of wallpaper – either lining paper or the reverse side of a patterned paper, the thicker the better. Do not use an embossed paper as nothing will stick to it.

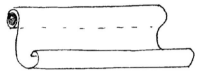

2 Measure the width of the altar and roll out the paper to match. You will need to cut two lengths to make up the height.

3 Stick the middle join together with glue and adjust the height at the middle by overlapping the two sheets of paper. Do not try to cut the paper at the bottom or top, as it is very difficult to cut a straight line. Be careful not to let the glue get on to the front.

4 Turn the paper over so the back is uppermost. Stick brown parcel tape along all the edges and across the middle join - this will stop the edges tearing and strengthen the paper when it is fixed to the altar.

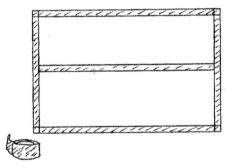

5 Think about how you are going to fix the altar frontal to the altar before you put the design on.

6 Now all you have to do is decorate the front.

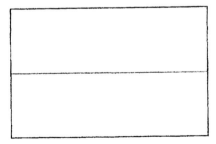

HOW TO PUT A DESIGN ON TO AN ALTAR FRONTAL

1 Decide what you want to say on the altar frontal. You might choose some words that are used in the service, like YOU SHALL NOT BE OVERCOME.
2 Think about the background. Will it be plain, or do you need to put a design on it before putting on the words?
3 Write the words on the computer using a program such as Word Art Gallery.
4 Remember that the words have to fit the space, so choose the font size carefully and think about the shape the words will make and therefore how they will be placed on the frontal.

5 Decide how you will put the words on the frontal.

a **Spray over the letters**. Cut out the letters and place them on the background, sticking them lightly with glue so they don't move when sprayed over. Spray over the letters. Carefully remove the letters, and the shapes of the letters will be left on the background.

b **Make a stencil and spray through the stencil**. Mark the letters on a large piece of paper in the shape you want them to be on the altar frontal. Carefully cut out the shapes of the letters using a craft knife. Put a small amount of glue on the back of the stencil to hold it in place. Place the stencil on background. Either spray through the stencil, or, using a stencil brush, paint over the stencil. Remove stencil and the letters will be on the background.

c **Cut out the letters in either paper or fabric and stick them on to the background**. Carefully mark where the letters will go before sticking them on. The letters should be made in a contrasting colour to the background so that they stand out well.

GOD CREATED HEAVEN AND EARTH

THANKS BE TO GOD

MAY THE
LIGHT OF CHRIST
SHINE IN OUR DARKNESS

HOW TO DECORATE AN ALTAR FRONTAL WITH BUTTERFLIES

You will need

1 Paper or fabric for the background – enough to fit the altar or table that it will go on.
2 A stencil brush.
3 Some fabric or poster paints.
4 A piece of card and a sharp knife.
5 Some spare paper to practise on.

What to do

1 Measure, cut out and neaten the edges of the background for the altar frontal.
2 Make a photocopy of the butterfly and cut out the shape.
3 Take a thick piece of card, place the cut-out butterfly shape on the card and draw around the butterfly shape.
4 Remove the paper butterfly and very carefully cut around the drawn butterfly shape using a small knife, only cutting round the lines of the butterfly shape – do not cut any other part of the card – so making a butterfly stencil.
5 You should then have a piece of card with a butterfly cut out of it.
6 Take a piece of paper and practise using the stencil and brush. Often one needs very little paint to get the best effect. Decide what colour or colours you want to use. Experiment making the butterflies in darker and lighter shades. They could be dark at the bottom of the design and get lighter as they go up the frontal. Think about where the butterflies should be positioned. There might be a large sun in the top of the design, as if the butterflies were flying to the light.
7 Now take the background for the altar frontal, and put your design on it.

HOW TO MAKE A STOLE

There are many shapes for stoles. They can vary in length and width and in the shape around the neck. For this purpose the shape will be kept as simple as possible, with the neck being shaped to fit the person the stole is being made for.

1 Decide on the width for the stole. About 4½ inches (12cm) would be a common width.

2 Cut out four pieces of fabric 6½ inches (17cm) wide. The length of the stole will depend on the height of the person who is going to wear it. It usually falls to about mid-shin on the person. The length will also be governed by how broad-shouldered the person is, so it may well be helpful to measure the person before cutting out the fabric.

3 Pieces 1 and 2 are for the front, 3 and 4 are for the back.

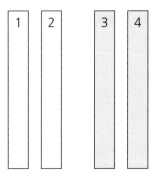

4 With right sides facing, place pieces 1 and 2 on top of each other. Pin and sew the neck as shown in the diagram. It would be good at this stage to fit the neck on the person the stole is being made for.

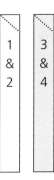

5 Repeat the same exercise with pieces 3 and 4.

6 Put the design onto the front pieces.

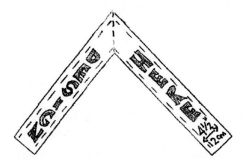

7 With right sides facing place pieces 1 and 2 on to pieces 3 and 4 and pin them together, making sure that the neck joins are placed together.

8 Sew up the sides of the pieces, making a long tube.

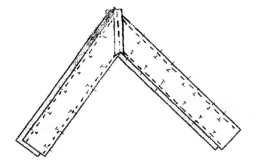

9 Turn the 'tube' inside out.

10 Press the edges with an iron.

11 Turn up the ends and stitch by hand.

BUTTERFLY STOLE

A butterfly emerging from a chrysalis is often used as an analogy for resurrection, breaking out of the tomb into freedom. A stole with a butterfly symbol on it can be very beautiful for a funeral. See how to make a stole on pages 178–179. Then decorate thus:

1 Place a cross either at the bottom or partway up the two sides of the stole. This can be spray-painted on or appliquéd, and should be done before painting on the butterflies.
2 Find a picture of a butterfly or use the template on page 176.
3 Photocopy it and make it gradually larger – the smaller butterflies are placed at the bottom of the stole, getting larger as they go up to the top.
4 Cut out stencils from the butterfly shapes.
5 Using either spray-paint or a stencil brush put the butterflies on to the stole (see pages 172 and 173).
6 Think about the colour of the butterflies. They might be darker at the bottom, becoming lighter as they progress up the stole.

ALTAR FRONTAL DESIGN FOR DESPAIR AND HOPE

FRONT SERVICE SHEET FOR A BABY OR YOUNG CHILD 1

A PRECIOUS CHILD IS BORN

IN
LOVING
MEMORY
OF
XXXXXX

A PRECIOUS CHILD HAS DIED

FRONT SERVICE SHEET FOR A BABY OR YOUNG CHILD 2

THE CHILD'S NAME
BORN
XXXX
DIED
XXXX

WHY?

O Lord, be with all who
despair and grieve

FRONT SERVICE SHEET FOR A BABY OR YOUNG CHILD 3

ALTAR FRONTAL DESIGN FOR JOURNEYING

ALTAR FRONTAL DESIGN FOR LOVE

HOW TO MAKE A PATCHWORK 'MEMORY' BANNER

This is a wonderful way to make a 'remembering' banner with a large group of people – family and/or friends of the person who has died. The idea is similar to a patchwork quilt. Each person makes his or her own 'patch' and then the whole thing is put together on to a common background. The patchwork can be made in fabric or paper. The patchwork can display photographs as well as pictures and text about the person who has died and their life. The background, whether it is made from fabric or paper, needs to be strong enough to hold the weight of all the patches. It might help to mount the whole thing on a light wooden frame or, if paper is used, put brown tape on the back around all the edges. This will give the edges more strength. Think about how the patches will be fixed to the background: They can be either glued on or sewn. When choosing glue, make sure to use one which will not mark the fabric if it is put on in the wrong place.

If people are not sure about sewing the patches on so that the stitches do not show, try to make the stitches big and bold as part of the design.

As well as being displayed in the church for the funeral, the patchwork can be given to the family to keep, so be aware that it will be handled and must be strong enough for this. Ask a small group of people to assemble the 'quilt'.

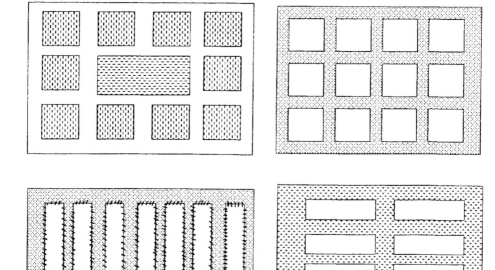

Fabric

- Everyone must be given a piece of fabric of the same size and weight to work on.
- The overall design can either be made by one person, or each person can make his or her own design.
- Some people might like to sew items on to their patch so the surface might be more three dimensional. Make sure it does not become too heavy.

Paper

- Everyone must be given a piece of paper of the same size and weight to work on.
- The overall design can either be made by one person, or each person can make his or her own design.
- Some people might like to stick items on to their patch so the surface might be more three dimensional. Make sure it does not become too heavy.

HOW TO MAKE A PAPER BOAT

1   Take a sheet of A4 paper and fold it in half from top to bottom.
2/3 Fold it in half the other way and make a good crease, then open it up again.
4   Fold the corners to the middle creased line with opening at bottom.
5/6 Fold the spare paper at the bottom up on each side.
7   Tuck the little flaps inside, take hold of the centre crease on each side, pull open
     and crease edges.
8   With the open edge at the bottom, fold the bottom point to the top. Turn over
     and repeat on the other side.
9   Holding the middle creases, open out and flatten the opposite way.
10   Take hold of the two top points and pull the boat open.

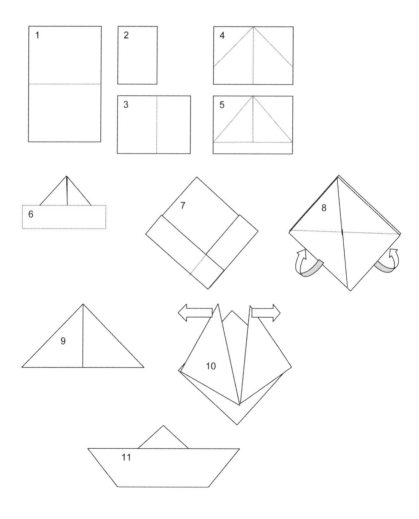

HOW TO PUT A DESIGN ON TO A CANDLE

Putting a design on to a candle is simple, but may need a little practice. Working on a rounded surface can be quite difficult the first time it is tried. Square candles are easier to work on. The bigger the candle, the easier it is to put on the design – very thin ones have little surface to work on.

1 First buy the candle, bearing in mind where it is to go and what the design is to be.
2 Decide on the colours to be used.
3 Work out the design to go on the candle, keeping it very simple.
4 Wrap a piece of paper round the candle to see how big the design should be and how it will be positioned on the candle. Most candles will only be seen from one side, so remember to design the candle with that in mind.
5 Now draw the design on the same piece of paper with a strong line. (If drawing is too difficult, use a computer to type and print off words in a big, bold font.)
6 Put clear adhesive tape onto the top and bottom of the design paper and stick in place on the candle.
7 With a ballpoint pen or pencil go over the design and gently press the design in to the candle surface.
8 Take the paper off the candle and the design should be visible on the surface.
9 With a waterproof felt pen, fill in the design.
10 Using relief outliner made to use on glass, go around the outline of the design.
11 Leave to dry.

ALTAR FRONTAL DESIGN FOR THE SEA 1

ALTAR FRONTAL DESIGN FOR THE SEA 2

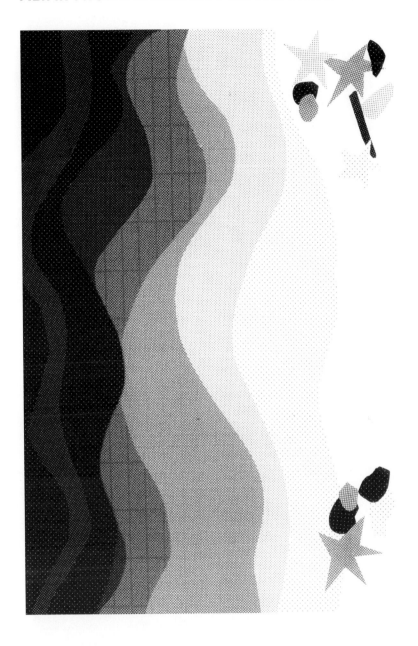

ALTAR FRONTAL DESIGN FOR THE SEA 3

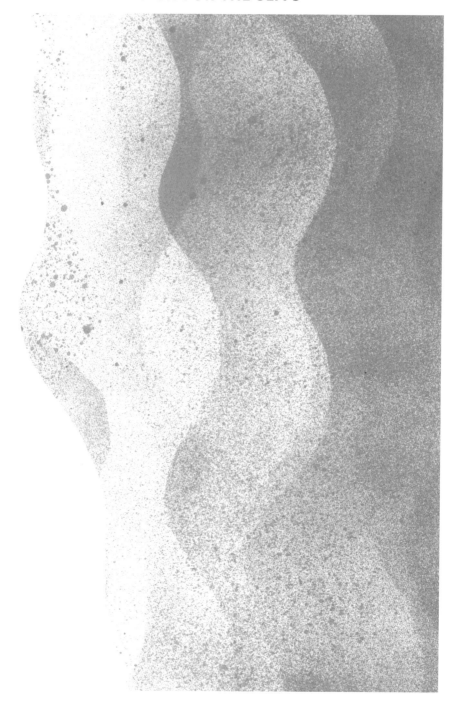

ALTAR FRONTAL DESIGN FOR VALLEYS AND MOUNTAINS

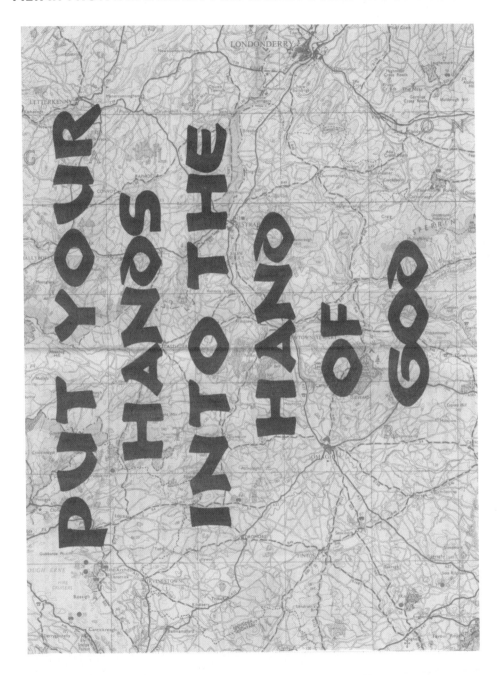

TEMPLATE OF DRAGONFLY FOR WATER BUGS AND DRAGONFLIES

WE
REMEMBER
WITH
LOVE

HOW TO MAKE A PAPER WATER LILY 1

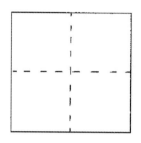

1 Open the paper napkin

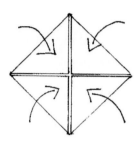

2 Fold corners in to the centre of napkin

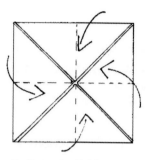

3 Repeat. Fold corners to centre

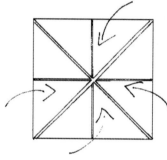

4 Turn napkin over and repeat, folding corners to centre

5 With one hand, hold the centre down. With the other hand, pull the corner petal from the back to the front, turning the petal inside out. Repeat with each corner

6 Pull the 'leaves' from the back to the front. You should now have a beautiful paper water lily

HOW TO MAKE A PAPER WATER LILY 2

You will need

- A sheet of yellow card for the centre of the flower.
- A sheet of cream card for the flower petals.
- Glue.
- Scissors.

1 Cut out two circles of yellow card, one slightly bigger than the other.

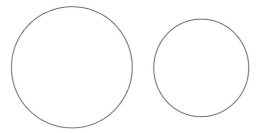

2 Cut out six water-lily flower petals in cream-coloured card. Make a half-inch (1.5cm) cut up into each petal as shown. Lift one side of the cut and stick over the other. This will make the petal 'stand up'.

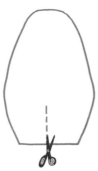

3 Stick the six petals round the edge of the larger of the card circles.

4 When all the petals are stuck on, stick the smaller of the circles over the large circle and petals, making this the inside of the flower.

5 Repeat and make as many flowers as you need.

TEMPLATES FOR WATER-LILY LEAVES FOR WATER BUGS AND DRAGONFLIES

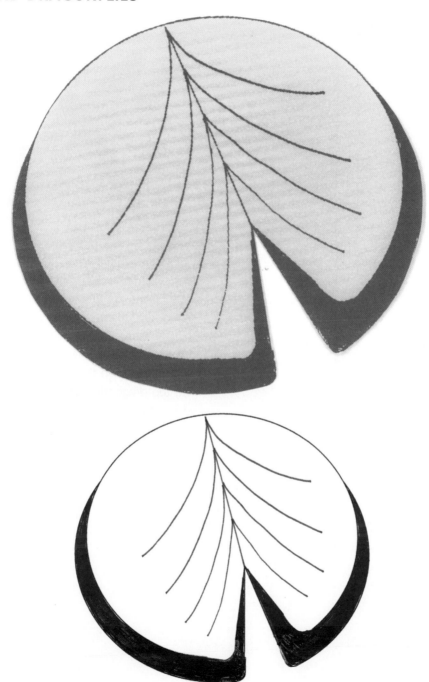

DESIGN FOR A DRAGONFLY STOLE

Cut a stencil of the dragonfly and, using fabric paints, stencil dragonflies up the stole. Cross the dragonflies from one side of the stole to the other, so giving them a sense of movement. Make the dragonflies at the bottom of the stole darker than the ones at the top. The top dragonfly could be golden. If you feel artistic, cut a stencil of some pondweed and stencil this onto the bottom of the stole before adding the dragonflies.

ALTAR FRONTAL DESIGN FOR WINTER AND SPRING 1

ALTAR FRONTAL DESIGN FOR WINTER AND SPRING 2

HOW TO MAKE A DRAWSTRING BAG TO HOLD ASHES

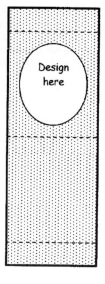

20cm long

12cm wide

1 Cut out a piece of fabric about 20cm long and 12cm wide.
2 If you are going to put a design on the bag, do it now.
3 Make a channel to take the string. Fold the fabric over about 5cm, on both of the short sides, iron it flat and sew along the bottom to make a channel.
4 With the right sides facing, fold the fabric in half in the centre, bringing the two short ends together.
5 Sew up the sides of the bag.
6 Turn the bag round the right way and press the seams flat.
7 Thread the string or cord through the two channels and tie the ends together.
8 Before the service, put the ashes in the bag.

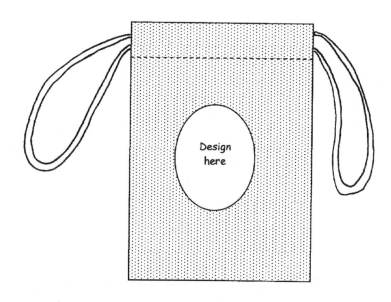

HOW TO MAKE AN EASEL FOR A CARD DISPLAY

You will need very stiff card cut into rectangular shapes large enough for the cards you want to display.

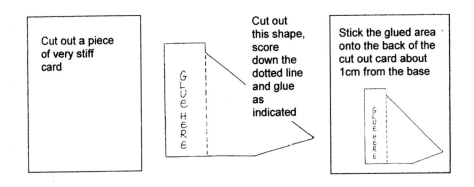

Cut out a piece of very stiff card

Cut out this shape, score down the dotted line and glue as indicated

Stick the glued area onto the back of the cut out card about 1cm from the base

Once the glue has dried, open the triangle and the card will stand up

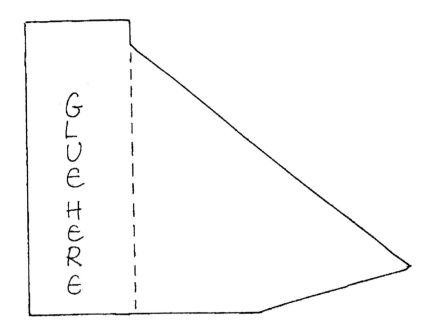

DESIGNS FOR MEMORIAL CARDS

WE REMEMBER

WITH LOVE

WE REMEMBER

WITH LOVE

WE REMEMBER

WITH LOVE

THE BOAT MAY SEEM VERY SMALL

BUT GOD'S LOVE IS VERY GREAT

WE REMEMBER   **WITH LOVE**

WE REMEMBER

WITH LOVE

WE REMEMBER

WITH LOVE

A SELECTION OF READINGS AND BLESSINGS

Authors are given where known.

A butterfly

A butterfly lights beside us like a sunbeam. And for a brief moment its glory and beauty belong to our world. But then it flies on again, and though we wish it could have stayed, we feel so lucky to have seen it . . .

Adrift
Tessa Wilkinson

My anchor has lost its hold
I am adrift
My boat is going where it will
The sails are tattered and torn
The sea seems enormous and uncharted
It throws me hither and thither
Into the deepest, darkest trough of despair
Then up into the sunlight and for a while there is hope
Then back again into the darkness
Will my little craft be overwhelmed?
As the huge waves of grief engulf it, will it come up again?
And again and again?
They say 'time heals . . .'
Can my little boat be trimmed out with new sails?
Can it sail again into a calm harbour and put down its anchor?
Can the navigation system be mended, so I know where I am going?
In time, in time . . .

but not yet.
This storm has to be passed through, and then a time will come to re-enter the harbour and return to still waters.

A flower bud
Tessa Wilkinson

A flower bud, holding so much beauty and expectation
Perfect in shape and colour and size
But sometimes it never opens.
So like a young child who dies
So beautiful in shape and form
Holding so many expectations for a future journey shared together
But it is a journey never to be taken
Never known
A journey which is cut off short and unfinished
A bud which never opened

After glow

I'd like the memory of me
to be a happy one.
I'd like to leave an after glow
of smiles when life is done.
I'd like to leave an echo
whispering softly down the ways,
Of happy times and laughing times
and bright and sunny days.
I'd like the tears of those who grieve,
to dry before the sun
of happy memories
that I leave when life is done.

A mother's lament
Tessa Wilkinson

I knew you every day as you grew
I felt your first movements as you stretched your growing limbs
You were cocooned in that safe warm world within me
protected and sheltered from the outside world
I met you on the scans and marvelled at your creation

I watched your life-giving heart beat
synchronised with mine

Now you are gone
No cries at birth, no phone calls of joy
Just stillness and silence
Your beautiful eyes never to open to look into mine
Your limbs still and lifeless as you enter this outside world
Your heart never to beat again
Your tiny fingers never to cling on
How I yearn to hold you in my arms
To fill the void, the emptiness

You are our child and we love you
Nothing can ever take that from us
We shall always remember you
Our *first/second* . . . precious child

A Navaho prayer

Grieve for me, for I would grieve for you
Then brush away the sorrow and the tears
Life is not over, but begins anew
With courage you must greet the coming years
To live forever in the past is wrong
It can only cause you misery and pain
Dwell not on memories overlong
With others you must share and care again
Reach out and comfort those who comfort you
Recall the years, but only for a while
Nurse not your loneliness; but live again
Forget not. Remember with a smile.

An old Gaelic blessing

May the road rise to meet you:
May the sun shine always on your face:
May the wind be always at your back:
May the rains fall gently on your fields:
And, until we meet again, may God keep you
In the hollow of his hand.

Bereavement
From *Watching for the Kingfisher*, Ann Lewin

Dark place
Where, vulnerable, alone,
We lick the wounds of loss.

Wise friends say little,
But hold us in their love,
And listen.

There are no guarantees,
Only reports from those
Who've been there,
That there is hope,
And life persists.

Birth is a beginning

Birth is a beginning
And death a destination
But life is a journey
A going – a growing
From stage to stage
From childhood to maturity
And youth to age
From innocence to awareness
And ignorance to knowing
From foolishness to discretion
And then perhaps, to wisdom
From weakness to strength
Or strength to weakness
And, often, back again
From health to sickness
And back, we pray, to health again
From offence to forgiveness
From loneliness to love
From joy to gratitude
From pain to compassion
And grief to understanding –
From fear to faith.

From defeat to defeat to defeat –
Until, looking backward or ahead,
We see that victory lies
Not as some high place along the way
But in having made the journey, stage by stage
A sacred pilgrimage
Birth is a beginning
And death a destination
But life is a journey
A sacred pilgrimage –
Made stage by stage –
To life everlasting.

Death
Rabindranath Tagore

Death is not the extinguishing of the light, but the putting out of the lamp because dawn has come.

Death of a partner
from *The Enduring Melody,* Michael Mayne

'Until death us do part.' If, within that closest of friendships, one should die, there is no greater anguish, no more lonely experience, than that of the one flesh being wrenched in two, with no one now to share the intimacies of your life, the private jokes and references. It's the heavy price we pay for loving, and our reason tells us that we would not have it otherwise, so that perhaps in time we may come to see that the grief we have to live with is the final, and most costly, gift we have to offer to the other who has died. But reason is not uppermost in periods of grief.

Firsts
Tessa Wilkinson

The journey of grief is one of 'firsts'
The first Birthday
The first Christmas
The first anniversary
The list is of endless firsts . . .
Each 'first' can loom ahead, huge, like a mountain to climb
A block on the way
But remember, once that 'first' is over it will never be a 'first' again

Next time we meet it, we will have met it before
We will know that that mountain can be climbed and we will start to believe that
we will be able to climb the next,
and the next, and the next . . .

From water bug to dragonfly
Tessa Wilkinson

The bottom of the pond is muddy and dark
There is fear of the unknown
There is loneliness as things change
There is the desperation of being left behind
Not knowing, not understanding
Watching and waiting
Then the journey comes
Up the stem
What waits beyond?
Sunlight
Freedom
Dancing together in joy with those who went before
And who will come after

God give them rest

'God give them rest in that delightful garden
where pain and grief are no more and sighing unknown.'

Grief

Grief is not for ever, but love is.

Grief
Tessa Wilkinson

Grief is like standing with your back to the sea
We never know when the big wave will come and knock us over

He did not say
Julian of Norwich

He did not say, 'You shall not be tempest-tossed, you shall not be work-weary, you
shall not be discomforted.' But he said, 'You shall not be overcome.' God wants

us to heed these words so that we shall always be strong in trust, both in sorrow and in joy.

He whom we love
St John Chrysostom

He whom we love and lose is no longer where he was before;
he is now wherever we are.

Henry's funeral
Tessa Wilkinson

When I saw the tiny coffin arrive it took my breath away. Coffins should be large and hold adults, and be carried by six strong men on their shoulders. Seeing that tiny shoebox-sized coffin being carried by one person was one of the most heartbreaking things I have ever seen.

I believe in the sun
Words found written on a cellar wall in Cologne after World War II

I believe in the sun even when it is not shining
I believe in love even when I feel it not
I believe in God even when he is silent.

I bind myself today

I bind myself today
The power of God to hold and lead
His eye to watch, His might to stay
His ear to hearken to my need
The wisdom of my God to teach
His hand to guide
His shield to ward
The word of God to give me speech
His heavenly Host to be my guide.

Ice
Tessa Wilkinson

The ice on the pond looks solid and sound
A tentative step onto the edge proves safe

Further out cracking noises beneath my feet
Deep threatening darkness below the ice
Fear, fast beating heart, run
Run back, back to the bank
To safety
To the place I know of solid rock.
So like visiting grief
Tiptoe to the edge of sadness and sorrow
Test the emotions, will they hold?
Will cracks appear, and the threat of breaking be too much to bear?
Will the place they might lead to be too dark and dangerous?
Will I trust I can make it back to my solid rock again?
Can I trust that all shall be well?

I dreamt that the time had come
Fernand de Vinck

I dreamt that the time had come to carry back to my Father the treasures I was
sent to gather on earth.
So I held out my chalice to my brother angel to be filled with the values of my
life.
I thought of bright achievement, renown and success,
but they vanished in the emptiness of glamour.
When it was handed back to me,
I found my cup filled to the brim with what I thought were tiny things,
hardly noticed and long forgotten,
but now, sparkling with the inner light of the love they contained.
Then I walked holding high the grail of my soul
and there was joy in heaven.

If
Corrie Ten Boom

If God sends us on stony paths he provides strong shoes.

If God brings you to it

If God brings you to it, he will bring you through it.
Happy moments, praise God.
Difficult moments, seek God.
Quiet moments, worship God.

Painful moments, trust God.
Every moment, thank God.

I have often wondered
Jan Brind

I have often wondered at this great mystery – that I, so small and insignificant, should have caught the attention of God? Strange that, just when I was feeling so empty and alone, God should beckon and say, 'Come to me – I will be with you. We will face this together.' I know now that God was always there, watching. But I was too busy with the humdrum things of life to notice. Oh, the joy of feeling that presence! And to know that God *is* always there – not just in sadness, but in the laughter and colour and busyness of life. Yes, God is always there – in life, and in death. And in the great adventure that is still to come.

I have seen death too often

I have seen death too often to believe in death.
It is not an ending, but a withdrawal.
As one who finishes a long journey,
Stills the motor,
Turns off the lights,
Steps from the car,
And walks up the path
To the home that awaits him.

In so much
St Augustine

In so much as love grows in you so in you beauty grows.
For love is the beauty of the soul.

Journey for a soul

Death is part of the future for everyone. It is the last post of this life and the reveille of the next. Death is the end of our present life, it is the parting from loved ones, it is the setting out into the unknown. We overcome death by accepting it as the will of a loving God, by finding him in it. Death, like birth, is only a transformation, another birth. When we die we shall change our state – that is all. And in faith in God, it is as easy and natural as going to sleep here and waking up there.

Lost love
Anne M. R. Chiles

A kiss never kissed
A dream never wished
An embrace never felt
A beauty never beheld
A tear never cried
A life never tried
A love never shown
A child never known.

Love
Tessa Wilkinson

You were conceived in love
Grew surrounded by our love
Died enfolded by love
Love never dies

Love is this

Love is this
That you lived among us these few years
And taught us love.

Love is this
That you died amongst us and helped us
To the source of life

With all our love
We wish you 'bon voyage'.

Love lives.

May the Warm Winds of Heaven

May the Warm Winds of Heaven
Blow softly upon your house
May the Great Spirit
Bless all who enter there
May your Moccasins

Make happy tracks
In many snows
And may the Rainbow
Always touch your shoulder.

People travel
St Augustine

People travel to wonder at the height of the mountains, at the huge waves of the sea, at the long courses of rivers, at the vast compass of the ocean, at the circular motion of the stars; and they pass by themselves without wondering.

Preparation for a journey
Tessa Wilkinson

When we know we are going on a journey
we pack our bag and get prepared:
A guide book to tell us where to visit
A map to show us the way
A torch to light the path
Food to sustain us
Water to refresh us
Clothes to keep us warm.
But for this journey there is no time to prepare:
Just get up and go, no time to think
No guide book to tell us where we should visit
No map to show the way through grief
The light seems to fade very fast
Food seems unpalatable
Water brings no refreshment.
Wrapped in sadness we feel we walk alone

Resurrection
from *Watching for the Kingfisher*, Ann Lewin

There are times when,
All being darkness and loss,
There is nothing for it
But to pick up your cross
And dance with it.

Snow
Tessa Wilkinson

The snow arrived unannounced
It overwhelmed everything
Changed the landscape so it was unrecognisable
No one was prepared
My grief feels like that snowstorm
I feel changed, weighed down by the burden
Trying to negotiate the new environment around me
Not knowing where I am going
Looking for familiar landmarks
I feel cold and miserable and ill equipped in this new place unvisited before
But I know in time the snow will melt and return the landscape to some semblance of normality
And I know in time my grief will diminish and I will find my way forward again, back to a world that I recognise, changed, but familiar
Spring does always come after winter and hope will return

So dead and yet so alive
Tessa Wilkinson

It looked dead, hanging upside down on the underside of the leaf
Motionless, a small sealed-up grey tomb
Seemingly doing nothing but just being there
Being there, doing nothing
Dead
But . . .
Gradually, gradually, something stirred
Was it movement?
How could it be when it looked so still and dead?
Then the grey tomb started to split
Little by little something began to emerge
Movement, struggle
Transforming death to life
To freedom, to beauty
To a butterfly

Support from others

Don't tell me that you understand.
Don't tell me that you know.
Don't tell me that I will survive,
How I will surely grow.
Don't come at me with answers
That can only come from me.
Don't tell me how my grief will pass,
That I will soon be free.
Accept me in my ups and downs.
I need someone to share.
Just hold my hand and let me cry
And say, 'My friend, I care.'

The calling
Jan Brind

Though we do not always walk in your Way
Or speak your Truth, or live your risen Life
And though we deny you over and over again
Still, Lord, you call us to be with you

When we think selfishly only of ourselves
And fail to see the needs of our neighbour
Or when we ignore the pain of your world around us
Still, Lord, you call us to be with you

Lord, you know us and call us by our name
And we are precious in your sight
You love us today, tomorrow and for all time
Knowing this – how can we hesitate?

Lord, we come to you with joy in our hearts

The End
Tessa Wilkinson

When an adult dies, it feels like the end of our past
But when a child dies it feels like the end of our future

The mountains of grief
Tessa Wilkinson

How can I possibly find a way over the mountains?
I have no map, I am weak and exhausted
The path is steep and stony, and very dark
I am afraid
I don't want to go on

The only way
Tessa Wilkinson

The only way we can be protected from the pain of loss and the grief we feel, is by having never loved. How empty our lives would be, and what a lot of wonderful shared moments we would have missed, if we had not known N. So, although what we feel at the moment is terrible, we must try to remember that it is because we have all been privileged to have known and loved N, that we now feel the pain and sadness.

The sea
Tessa Wilkinson

The sea is such a fickle thing
One minute smooth and calm
Blue and tranquil
The next rough and raging
Tossing anything in its path up in the air
Throwing it where it will.
So like grief
One minute we feel calm
'Today I am all right'
'Today I will not be battered and tossed about not knowing where or who I am'
Then we see something
Or hear something
Or smell something
Quite out of the blue
And the wall of grief that we thought we had turned from
Picks us up and tosses us here and there
Until we land exhausted back on the shore

The sea and the beach
Tessa Wilkinson

The sea seems to illustrate pain and sorrow so well
It comes in and goes out
For a while it is there, overwhelming, covering everything
Then slowly the tide turns and it withdraws
For a while we can see the beauty of the shells, the seaweed
We can rejoice in the patterns in the sand
We can feel the corrugated ripples under our feet
Alive to what is around, and beyond
But then the tide turns and again it is all washed away, all overwhelmed
We feel like the crashing of the waves on rocks
Raw and out of control
Full of anger and rage
Battered and bruised
Tossed about like flotsam floating wherever we are thrown
There are so many questions. *Why now? Why her?*
But no answers
Then the sea calms and gently the waves lap the rocks
We are soothed and the inner turmoil is calmed
In time we can learn to move up the beach as the tide comes in
Out of its reach
Not to be overwhelmed
The pain is still there, but in control
We can recognise the pain
Revisiting the sadness
Acknowledging how much the person is missed
We learn to turn away and look to the future
Knowing the person will always be part of us
Always loved and always remembered

Tomb
from *Watching for the Kingfisher*, Ann Lewin

The place of remembering:
Where as the work of grief is done,
Memory recovers its perspective.

Letting the dead one go,
With aching sense of loss,

Opens the way to finding again
A rounded person, gifts and faults
Delights and irritations;
Makes it possible to share again
The jokes, the intimate glance,
Keep company unseen.

We can
Tessa Wilkinson

We can climb the highest mountains
We can visit the darkest valleys
Along the way we may feel lost, hopeless and afraid
But with friends walking beside us
We will find the way through grief
And arrive at last feeling joy in our hearts again

We can shed tears that they have gone

We can shed tears that they have gone,
or we can smile that they have lived
We can close our eyes and pray that they will come back
or we can open our eyes and see all the good that they have left us
Our hearts can be empty because we cannot see them
or our hearts can be full with the love that we've shared
We can turn our backs on tomorrow and live yesterday
or we can be happy for tomorrow, *because* of yesterday
We can remember them and only that they have gone
or we can cherish their memory and let it live on
We can cry and close our minds,
be empty and turn our backs
or we can do what they would have wanted:
smile, open our eyes, love and go on.

We grieve your heart, O God
Jan Brind

We grieve your heart, O God
When we disrespect the world you have given us
So freely
We grieve your heart, O God,

When we cover your earth with concrete
Trapping seeds that bring new growth
We grieve your heart, O God
When we tear down your forests
Which anchor the land and shade us
We grieve your heart, O God
When we pollute the water
That should revive and refresh
We grieve your heart, O God
When we fill the air with poisonous fumes
So that your living things suffocate
We grieve your heart, O God
When we dump our unwanted rubbish in your oceans
So that the fish and creatures of the sea are harmed
We grieve your heart, O God
When we see injustice and poverty
And do nothing
We grieve your heart, O God
When we fail to love our brothers and sisters
As you have commanded
We grieve your heart, O God
Oh, how we grieve your heart

Forgive your people, O God, and change us
Soften our hearts
And breathe new life into us
Lead us in your ways of love and truth
That we may care for your creation
And renew the face of the earth

We must live through the dreary winter

We must live through the dreary winter
If we would value the spring;
And the woods must be cold and silent
Before the robins sing.
The flowers must be buried in darkness
Before they can bud and bloom,
And the sweetest, warmest sunshine
Comes after the storm and gloom.

We trust

We trust that beyond absence there is a presence.
That beyond the pain there can be healing.
That beyond the brokenness there can be wholeness.
That beyond the anger there may be peace.
That beyond the hurting there may be forgiveness.
That beyond the silence there may be the word.
That beyond the word there may be understanding.
That through understanding there is love.

When I die and leave behind

When I die and leave behind
This earth I love
These trees, this sky
The pounding sea
The yearly hope of spring
Cry not for me
Rejoice
My soul has wings
And in its freedom sings.

When loving someone is not enough
Jan Brind

The phone rings . . . the voice at the other end sounds nervous. There is dreadful news. Shocking news that no one should ever have to give, or receive. *He is dead. He has taken his own life. He was found this afternoon.* In that moment the world is changed and time is suspended. A dreadful silent scream 'No! No! No!' explodes inside me and yet, and yet, with a terrible realisation and certainty, I know it is true. Why didn't he 'phone? He promised he would. Last conversations are remembered and replayed over and over, word for word. What did we miss?

But, sadly, loving someone is not always enough. His pain was such that, for him, dying was an easier option than living. And now we are left, in this place where he is no longer. With the 'If onlys', and the 'What ifs', and a huge sadness and regret that someone we loved and cherished chose not to stay with us, but to go. Such truth is hard to accept. But this we do believe. He is at peace now and his pain is no more. He is with God in a place where all things are made well and where all darkness is overcome. Slowly our pain, too, will be healed, and we will remember him as he was before, embracing life to the full and laughing with the joy of it. And we will smile again at the memory and hold it in our hearts.

Winter and spring

When winter comes, spring will not be far behind.

A SELECTION OF RESOURCE BOOKS

These might be helpful when planning funerals, memorials and thanksgivings.

A Wee Worship Book, Wild Goose Worship Group, Wild Goose Publications, 1999.

All in the End is Harvest: An anthology for those who grieve, edited by Agnes Whitaker, Darton, Longman and Todd, 1984.

Approaches to Prayer: A resource book for groups and individuals, edited by Henry Morgan, SPCK, 1991.

Badger's Parting Gifts, Susan Varley, Picture Lions, 1992.

Bread for the Journey: Reflections for every day of the year, Henri J. M. Nouwen, Darton, Longman and Todd, 1996.

Common Worship: Pastoral Services 2nd edition, Liturgical Commission, Church House Publishing, 2004.

Coping with Suicide, Maggie Helen, Sheldon Press, 2002.

Crafts for Creative Worship: A resource and activity book for parishes, Jan Brind and Tessa Wilkinson, Canterbury Press, 2004.

Creating Uncommon Worship, Richard Giles, Canterbury Press, 2004.

Creative Ideas for Evening Prayer: For seasons, feasts and special occasions, Jan Brind and Tessa Wilkinson, Canterbury Press, 2005.

Do Not Go Gentle: Poems for funerals, edited by Neil Astley, Bloodaxe Books, 2003.

Enfolded in Love: Daily readings with Julian of Norwich, Julian of Norwich, Darton, Longman and Todd, 1980.

Funerals: A guide – prayers, hymns and readings, James Bentley, Andrew Best and Jackie Hunt, Hodder & Stoughton, 1994.

Funerals in the Church of England, The Archbishops' Council, (Leaflet) Church House Publishing, 2003.

Give Sorrow Words, Susan Walter, Redemptorist Publications, 1998.

Holy Ground: Liturgies and worship resources for an engaged spirituality, Neil Paynter and Helen Boothroyd, Wild Goose Publications, 2005.

I'll Always Love You, Hans Wilhelm, Crown Publications, 1988.

In Sure and Certain Hope, Paul Sheppy, Canterbury Press, 2003.

In This Hour – Liturgies for Pausing, Dorothy McRae-McMahon, SPCK, 2001.

Iona Abbey Worship Book, compiled by The Iona Community, Wild Goose Publications, 2001.

Liturgies for the Journey of Life, Dorothy McRae-McMahon, SPCK, 2000.

Making Liturgy: Creating rituals for worship and life, edited by Dorothea McEwan, Pat Pinsent, Ianthe Pratt and Veronica Seddon, Canterbury Press, 2001.

Multi-sensory Prayer, Sue Wallace, Scripture Union, 2000.

New Patterns for Worship, The Archbishops' Council, Church House Publishing, 2002.

Out of the Ordinary: Prayers, poems and reflections for every season, Joyce Rupp, Ave Maria Press, 2000.

Poems and Readings for Funerals, edited by Julia Watson, Penguin Books, 2004.

Prayer After Abortion, edited by Althea Hayton, Wren Publications, 1997.

Prayer Rhythms: Fourfold patterns for each day, Ray Simpson, Kevin Mayhew, 2003.

Prayers Encircling The World: An international anthology of 300 contemporary prayers, compiled by SPCK, SPCK, 1998.

Prayers for Life's Particular Moments, Dorothy McRae-McMahon, SPCK, 2001.

Present On Earth: Worship resources on the life of Jesus, Wild Goose Worship Group, Wild Goose Resource Group, Wild Goose Publications, 2002.

Rainbows Through Clouds, edited by Janet Glover, Lady Glover, 1997.

Seeing Christ In Others, edited by Geoffrey Duncan, Canterbury Press, 2002.

Stages On The Way: Worship resources for Lent, Holy Week and Easter, Wild Goose Worship Group, Wild Goose Resource Group, Wild Goose Publications, 1998.

The Death of a Child, Tessa Wilkinson, Julia McRae Books, 1991.

The Enduring Melody, Michael Mayne, Darton, Longman and Todd, 2006.

The Funeral Services Book, Canterbury Press, 2003.

The Gates of Prayer, Central Conference, 1996.

The Long Pale Corridor: Contemporary poems on bereavement, edited by Judi Benson and Agneta Falk, Bloodaxe Books, 1996.

The Nation's Favourite Poems of Remembrance, foreword by Michel Rosen, BBC Books, 2003.

The Natural Death Handbook, Josefine Speyer and Stephanie Weinrich of the Natural Death Centre, Rider & Co., 2003.

The Prophet, Kahlil Gibran, Pan Books, 1991.

The Rhythm Of Life: Celtic Daily Prayer, David Adam, SPCK, 1996.

The Shade Of His Hand: Prayers and readings in times of sorrow and times of joy, Michael Hollings and Etta Gullick, Hodder & Stoughton, 1975.

The Very Hungry Caterpillar, Eric Carle, Puffin Books, 2002.

Using Common Worship – Funerals, R Anne Horton, Church House Publishing and Praxis, 2000.

Watching for the Kingfisher, Ann Lewin, Inspire, 2004.

Water Bugs and Dragonflies: Explaining death to children, Doris Stickney, Mowbray, 1982.

Words by the Way, Ann Lewin, Inspire, 2005.

Words to Comfort and Words to Heal: Poems and meditations for those who grieve, compiled by Juliet Mabey, Oneworld Publications, 1998.

You Visited Me, Susan Hardwick, Kevin Mayhew, 1997.

HYMNS AND SONGS

Be Still and Know

Be still, my soul
Calm me, Lord
Day is done, but love unfailing
Do not be afraid
Going home
I heard the voice of Jesus say
In God alone my soul
In the darkness of the still night
May the Lord bless you
May you walk with Christ beside you
Silent, surrendered
The Lord is my light (Taizé)
We walk by faith

Cantate

Bambelela
Be with me, Lord
Kyrie
Let us go in peace
My peace I leave you

Celebration Hymnal for Everyone

Eye has not seen

Celtic Hymn Book

Come, my Lord, my light, my way
Come to me

Empty, broken, here I stand
Holy Weaver, may we watch you
I am tired and I a stranger
In my Father's house
Jesus, draw me ever nearer
Kindle a flame
Lord, I cry to you
Put peace into each other's hands
Teach me, dear Lord
The tide ebbs
Through the love of God our saviour

Children's Praise

Care for one another
Father be with her family
Father for our friends we pray

Christ, Be Our Light

O God, you search me
Your words are spirit and life

Church Hymnary

Give thanks for life, the measure of our days
God in his love for us lent us this planet
God of the living, in whose eyes
Hear me, dear Lord, in this my time of sorrow
In the bulb there is a flower
Today I live, one day shall come my death
Touch the earth lightly
When Jesus longed for us to know
When we are living, we are in the Lord

Common Ground

Come to me
Comfort, comfort now my people
Final Commendation
God give us life
Hear me, dear Lord

Complete Anglican Hymns Old and New

O what their joy and their glory must be
The Lord is my light (Margaret Rizza)
There's a wideness in God's mercy

Go Before Us

Go before us
My soul is thirsting

God Beyond All Names

God, beyond all names
O God, for you I long

Heaven Shall Not Wait

Oh where are you going?

Hymns Ancient and Modern Revised

Guide me, O thou great redeemer

Hymns Old and New – New Anglican Edition

Dear Lord and Father of mankind
Eternal Father, strong to save
Father, hear the prayer we offer
Give us the wings of faith
God moves in a mysterious way
Lead us, heavenly Father, lead us
Let there be love
Lord of all hopefulness
Now the green blade riseth
Spirit of the living God
Think of a world without any flowers

Hymns Old and New: One Church, One Faith, One Lord

Abide with me
All who would valiant be
Be thou my vision
Brother, sister, let me serve you
Faithful vigil ended

From the falter of breath
Give thanks for those
Go peaceful, in gentleness
Immortal love, for ever full
In heavenly love abiding
Jesus put this song
Lord, I come to you (The power of your love)
O Lord, my God, when I in awesome wonder
Saviour, again to thy dear name we raise
Thanks be to God
The King of love my shepherd is
The Lord's my shepherd
Thine be the glory

Iona Abbey Music Book

God to enfold you
Will you come and follow me

Laudate

As the deer pants for the water
Healer of our every ill
I know that my redeemer lives (Stephen Dean)
May flights of angels
Since we are summoned
Sing with all the saints in glory
Song of Farewell

Restless is the Heart

Everyday God
Unless a grain of wheat

Sing Glory

Because the Lord is my shepherd
Here from all nations, all tongues
Jesus, your blood and righteousness
Rock of ages, cleft for me
Then I saw a new heaven

Songs From Taizé

Bless the Lord, my soul
Jesus, remember me
Lord Jesus Christ
Nothing can trouble (Nada te turbe)
Within our darkest night

The Children's Hymn Book

All things bright and beautiful
Caterpillar, caterpillar
Father, I place into your hands
If I were a butterfly
Lord, the light of your love (Shine, Jesus, shine)
Morning has broken
One more step along the world I go

There is One Among Us

Lo, I am with you
The peace of the earth

Turn My Heart

O God, why are you silent?
Turn my heart
Watch, O Lord

When Grief is Raw

A cradling song
Christ's is the world (A touching place)
For all the saints who showed your love
Go, silent friend
I cry to God
Let your restless hearts be still
O Christ, you wept
There is a place
We cannot care for you the way we wanted
We cannot measure

MUSIC SUPPLEMENT

God is making all things new

1 Though our tears may last the night
   Sorrow putting sleep to flight
   While our dreams are far and few
   God is making all things new
   Joy will come with morning dew
   God is making all things new

2 Though confusion leads to fear
   Things once veiled are now made clear
   What was false is now made true
   God is making all things new
   We recall and we review
   God is making all things new

3 Shades of memories unwind
   Painting pictures in our mind
   Colours rich in every hue
   God is making all things new
   Love and hope are woven through
   God is making all things new

Text © Jan Brind 2006
Music © David Davies 2006
This song can also be sung to Heathlands 77 77 77

God is making all things new

Jan Brind

David Davies

Though our tears may last the night, sor - row put - ting sleep__ to flight__ while_ our

dreams are far and few: God__ is ma__ king all__ things new. Joy will

come with morn - ing dew: God__ is ma__ king all things new.

Jan Brind & David Davies

Song during a time of grief

1 Lord, we pray, be near us,
   In this time of grief;
   Bring us peace and healing,
   Solace and relief:
   Heaviness surrounds us
   Like a storm-filled cloud;
   Sounds of day and sunlight
   Now seem harsh and loud.

2 As the shadows deepen
   Chasing out the light;
   Hold us in your hand, and
   Lead us through the night:
   May we, in our sorrow,
   Feel your loving care;
   When life overwhelms us
   Know that you are near.

3 In the end we trust that
   All shall be made well;
   Send your Holy Spirit
   In our hearts to dwell:
   Gently, oh so gently,
   Day must dawn again;
   Shafts of golden sunlight
   Shining through the rain.

Song during a time of grief

Jan Brind

David Davies

Lord we pray be near us   in this time of grief;   bring us peace and heal - ing,   so-lace and re -

lief: hea - vi - ness sur - rounds   us   like a storm-filled cloud;

sounds   of   day   and   sun - light   now seem harsh and   loud.

Song of yearning

Tune Song of Yearning 77 77 7

1 Holy God, to you we cry
   Broken souls in anguish sigh
   Calm our hearts and make us strong
   Soothe the sorrow of our song
   Soothe the sorrow of our song

2 Like a shepherd you will seek
   For the lost, the low, the meek
   Guide our steps and lead us on
   Bear the sorrow of our song
   Bear the sorrow of our song

3 Gentle Jesus, draw us near
   Speak the words which quell our fear
   Bring the peace for which we long
   Heal the sorrow of our song
   Heal the sorrow of our song

4 Shining Spirit warm and bright
   Turn our darkness into light
   By your power we'll be reborn
   In the music of your song
   In the music of your song

Song of Yearning

Words and Music by Jan Brind

Ho - ly God to you we cry, bro - ken souls in an - guish sigh, calm our hearts and make us strong, soothe the sor - row of __ our song, soothe the sor - row of __ our song.

Song of Yearning

Jan Brind

David Davies

Ho - ly God, to you we cry bro - ken souls in an - guish sigh, calm our hearts and make us strong, __ soothe the sor - row of our song, soothe the sor - row of our song.

SELECTION OF HYMN BOOKS AND SONG BOOKS

CDs or cassettes are available for titles marked with an asterisk

Be Still and Know, compiled by Margaret Rizza, Kevin Mayhew, 2000.

Beneath a Travelling Star, Timothy Dudley-Smith, Canterbury Press, 2001.

Cantate: A book of short chants, hymns, responses and litanies, edited by Stephen Dean, Decani Music, 2005.

Celebration Hymnal for Everyone, edited by Patrick Geary, McCrimmons, 1994.

Celtic Hymn Book, selected by Ray Simpson, Kevin Mayhew, 2005.

Children's Praise, compiled by Greg Leavers and Phil Burt, Marshall Pickering, 1991.

*Christ, Be Our Light, Bernadette Farrell, OCP Publications, 1994 (available from Decani Music).

Church Hymnary (4th edition), Editorial panel convened by the Church of Scotland and led by John L. Bell and Charles Robertson, Canterbury Press, 2005.

*Come All You People: Shorter songs for worship, John L. Bell, Wild Goose Publications, 1994.

*Common Ground: A song book for all the churches, John L. Bell and Editorial Committee, Saint Andrew Press, 1998.

Common Praise, compiled by Hymns Ancient & Modern Ltd, Canterbury Press, 2000.

Complete Anglican Hymns Old and New, compiled by Geoffrey Moore, Susan Sayers, Michael Forster and Kevin Mayhew, Kevin Mayhew, 2000.

*Drawn to the Wonder: hymns and songs from churches worldwide, compiled by Francis Brienen and Maggie Hamilton, Council for World Mission, 1995.

Enemy of Apathy, John L. Bell and Graham Maule, Wild Goose Publications, 1988 (revised 1990).

*Fire of Love, Margaret Rizza, Kevin Mayhew, 1998.

*Fountain of Life, Margaret Rizza, Kevin Mayhew, 1997.

Gather (2nd edition), edited by Robert J. Batastini, GIA Publications, 1994.

*Gift of God, Marty Haugen, GIA Publications, 2001.

Glory and Praise (2nd Edition), Oregon Catholic Press, 2000.

*Go Before Us, Bernadette Farrell, OCP Publications, 2003 (available from Decani Music).

*God Beyond all Names, Bernadette Farrell, OCP Publications, 1991 (available from Decani Music).

*Heaven Shall Not Wait, John L. Bell and Graham Maule, Wild Goose Publications, 1987 (reprinted 1994).

Hymns and Psalms, British Methodist Conference, Methodist Publishing House, 1987.

Hymns Old and New – New Anglican Edition, compiled by Geoffrey Moore, Susan Sayers, Michael Forster and Kevin Mayhew, Kevin Mayhew, 1996.

Hymns Old and New: One Church, One Faith, One Lord, compiled by Colin

Mawby, Kevin Mayhew, Susan Sayers, Ray Simpson and Stuart Thomas, Kevin Mayhew, 2004.

I Will Not Sing Alone, John L. Bell, Wild Goose Publications, 2004.

Innkeepers and Light Sleepers: Songs for Christmas, John L. Bell, Wild Goose Publications, 1992.

Iona Abbey Music Book: Songs from the Iona Abbey Worship Book, compiled by The Iona Community, Wild Goose Publications, 2003.

Light In Our Darkness, Margaret Rizza, Kevin Mayhew, 2002.

Laudate, edited by Stephen Dean, Decani Music, 2000.

Liturgical Hymns Old and New, compiled by Robert Kelly, Sister Sheila McGovern SSL, Kevin Mayhew, Father Andrew Moore and Sister Louisa Poole SSL, Kevin Mayhew, 1999.

Love and Anger: Songs of lively faith and social justice, John L. Bell and Graham Maule, Wild Goose Publications, 1997.

Love from Below, John L. Bell and Graham Maule, Wild Goose Publications, 1989.

Many and Great: World Church songs Vol. 1, John L. Bell and Graham Maule, Wild Goose Publications, 1990.

Methodist Hymns Old and New, compiled by Revd Peter Bolt, Revd Amos Cresswell, Mrs Tracy Harding and Revd Ray Short, Kevin Mayhew, 2001.

Mission Praise, compiled by Roland Fudge, Peter Horrobin and Greg Leavers, Marshall Pickering, 1983.

New Hymns And Worship Songs, Kevin Mayhew, 2001.

New Start Hymns And Songs, compiled by Kevin Mayhew, Kevin Mayhew, 1999.

One is the Body: Songs of unity and diversity, John L. Bell, Wild Goose Publications, 2002.

Psalms of Patience, Protest and Praise: 23 psalm settings, John L. Bell, Wild Goose Publications, 1993.

Rejoice and Sing, Oxford University Press, 1991.

Restless is the Heart, Bernadette Farrell, OCP Publications, 2000 (available from Decani Music).

Resurrexit: music for Lent, the Easter Triduum and Eastertide, edited by Stephen Dean, Decani Music, 2001.

River of Peace, Margaret Rizza, Kevin Mayhew, 1998.

Sacred Dance: Celtic music from Lindisfarne, Keith Duke, Kevin Mayhew, 2005.

Sacred Pathway: Celtic songs from Lindisfarne, Keith Duke, Kevin Mayhew, 2004.

Sacred Weave: Celtic songs from Lindisfarne, Keith Duke, Kevin Mayhew, 2003.

Sent by the Lord: World Church songs Vol. 2, John L. Bell and Graham Maule, Wild Goose Publications, 1991.

Share the Light, Bernadette Farrell, OCP Publications, 2000 (available from Decani Music).

Sing! New Words for Worship, Rosalind Brown, Jeremy Davies and Ron Green, Sarum College Press, 2004.

Sing Glory: Hymns, psalms and songs for a new century, edited by Michael Baughen, Kevin Mayhew, 1999.

Songs and Prayers From Taizé, Ateliers et Presses de Taizé, Geoffrey Chapman Mowbray, 1991 (Reprinted 1992).

Songs of God's People, The Panel on Worship, Church of Scotland, Oxford University Press, 1988 (Reprinted 1995).

Songs from Taizé, Ateliers et Presses de Taizé, Ateliers et Presses de Taizé, published annually.

Songs of Fellowship, compiled by members of Kingsway Music Editorial Team, Kingsway Music, 1991.

Taizé: Songs for Prayer (Instrumental Edition), Ateliers et Presses de Taizé, HarperCollins, 2001.

Taizé: Songs for Prayer (Vocal Edition), Ateliers et Presses de Taizé, HarperCollins, 1998

Tales of Wonder, Marty Haugen, GIA Publications, 1989 (available from Decani Music).

The Children's Hymnbook, compiled by Kevin Mayhew, Kevin Mayhew, 1997.

The Courage to Say No: Songs for Lent and Easter, John L. Bell and Graham Maule, Wild Goose Publications, 1996.

The Last Journey: Reflections for the time of grieving, John L. Bell, Wild Goose Publications, 1996.

The New English Hymnal, compiled by Anthony Caesar, Christopher Dearnley, Martin Draper, Michael Fleming, Arthur Hutchings, Colin Roberts and George Timms, Canterbury Press, 1986 (reprinted 1999).

The Source 3: Definitive worship collection, compiled by Graham Kendrick, Kevin Mayhew, 2005.

There is One Among Us: Shorter songs for worship, John L. Bell, Wild Goose Publications, 1998.

Turn My Heart: Praying the sacred journey from brokenness to healing, Marty Haugen, GIA Publications, 2003 (available from Decani Music).

Veni Emmanuel: Music for Advent and Christmastide, edited by Stephen Dean, Decani Music, 2001.

* *Walk With Christ*, Stephen Dean, OCP Publications, 1996 (available from Decani Music).

When Grief Is Raw: Songs for times of sorrow and bereavement, John L. Bell and Graham Maule, Wild Goose Publications, 1997.

World Praise, David Peacock and Geoff Weaver, Marshall Pickering, 1993.

Worship (3rd edition), edited by Robert J. Batastini, GIA Publications Inc., 1986.

21st Century Folk Hymnal, compiled by Kevin Mayhew, Kevin Mayhew, 1999.

USEFUL CDS

Across the Blue Sea
Celtic reflections
Simeon Wood
Eagle

The Armed Man: A Mass for Peace
Karl Jenkins
Virgin Records

Be Still My Soul
Music for prayer and quiet times
Colin Mawby
Kevin Mayhew Ltd

The Celtic Spirit
Poems, prayers and music
Lion Publishing

Cradle Song
The music of Schumann, Dvořák, Rutter, Fauré and others
Julian Lloyd Webber and John Lenehan
Kevin Mayhew Ltd

Dreamcatcher
Secret Garden
Philips

Icons 1
Instrumental music
Margaret Rizza
Kevin Mayhew Ltd

Majors for Minors
Classical music nursery rhymes
Newsound 2000

Music for Funeral and Memorial Services
Choral and instrumental music
Kevin Mayhew Ltd

Music for Solemn Moments
Harrison Oxley and Noel Rawsthorne
Kevin Mayhew Ltd

Requiem
Karl Jenkins
EMI Classics

Sanctuary
Christian Forshaw
Quartz Music

USEFUL WEBSITES

Coffins, caskets and burials

www.crosswayswoodlandburials.co.uk
Woodland burial site in Devon. Biodegradable coffins and caskets in willow,
bamboo, papier-maché and pine.

www.greenburialsite.co.uk
Biodegradable willow, bamboo and cardboard coffins and caskets.

www.memorialcentre.co.uk/coffincover
Wooden outer cover containing biodegradable inner coffin. Only the inner
coffin is buried or cremated. Also wicker coffins.

www.memorialwoodlands.com
Multi-faith and ecological funerals.

www.nativewoodland.co.uk
Lists the woodland and natural burial sites in the UK.

www.naturaldeath.org.uk
Natural burial grounds.

www.naturalendings.co.uk
Environmentally friendly coffins made from willow, bamboo, wicker,
ecopods, cardboard and reclaimed timber. Woodland sites. North West of
England.

www.peacefunerals.co.uk
Woodland cemeteries in Yorkshire and Derbyshire. Wicker coffins and
caskets. Railway funerals.

www.thegreenfuneralcompany.co.uk
Environmentally friendly.

Doves

www.dovesrus.co.uk (Essex)
www.thewhitedovecompany.co.uk
www.wingsoflove.co.uk (North West England)

Fireworks

www.fantasticfireworks.co.uk
www.heavensabovefireworks.com

Jewellery

www.lifegem.com

Poems, readings and resources

www.cofe.anglican.org/worship/liturgy/commonworship/texts/funeral/
funeralfront.html
www.goodgriefresources.com
www.grieflossrecovery.com
www.griefsjourney.com
www.griefwatch.com
www.jfda.org/povg.html
www.journeyofhearts.org
www.poeticexpressions.co.uk
www.quoteworld.org
www.rfgifts.com
www.words-of-sympathy.com

Stars

www.memorialstars.com

Support groups

Alzheimer's Disease Association
Offering support to those coping with dementia.
www.alzheimers.org.uk

Compassionate Friends
Support for bereaved parents and their families.
www.tcf.org.uk

Cruse
Support for those who are bereaved.
www.crusebereavementcare.org.uk

Miscarriage Association
Offering support and understanding.
www.miscarriageassociation.org.uk

SANDS
Stillbirth and Neonatal Death Society.
www.uk-sands.org

SOBS
Survivors of bereavement by suicide.
www.uk-sobs.org.uk

ACKNOWLEDGEMENTS

A Reflective Quiet Time After a Miscarriage

'Lost Love' copyright © Anne M. R. Chiles 2000, and used with permission from the Miscarriage Association.

A Selection of Readings and Blessings

'Resurrection' taken from *Watching for the Kingfisher* copyright © Ann Lewin 2004, published by Inspire and used with the author's permission.

A Selection of Readings and Blessings

'Tomb' taken from *Watching for the Kingfishe*r copyright © Ann Lewin 2004, published by Inspire and used with the author's permission.

After a Death by Suicide

Extract from *The Shade of his Hand* by Michael Hollings and Etta Gullick copyright © McCrimmons, Great Wakering, Essex SS3 0EQ, and used with permission.

After the Sudden Death of a Young Adult

Extracts from *Common Worship: Services and Prayers for the Church of England* and from *Common Worship: Pastoral Services* are copyright © The Archbishops' Council 2000, and are reproduced by permission.

Despair and Hope

'Bereavement' taken from *Watching for the Kingfisher* copyright © Ann Lewin 2004, published by Inspire and used with the author's permission.

Original Music

Original music for 'God is making all things new', 'Holy God, to you we cry', and 'Lord, we pray be near us' composed by David Davies, Sub-organist at Guildford Cathedral, with grateful thanks.